CSI
ALBERTA

CSI
ALBERTA

The Secrets of Skulls and Skeletons

PETER B. SMITH

VICTORIA · VANCOUVER · CALGARY

Heritage House Publishing Company Ltd.
heritagehouse.ca

CATALOGUING INFORMATION AVAILABLE FROM LIBRARY AND ARCHIVES CANADA

978-1-894974-84-4 (pbk)
978-1-926936-16-1 (epub)

Series editor: Lesley Reynolds.
Cover design: Chyla Cardinal. Interior design: Frances Hunter.
Cover photo: Stefan Klein/iStockphoto.

The interior of this book was produced on 30% post-consumer recycled paper, processed chlorine free and printed with vegetable-based inks.

We acknowledge the financial support of the Government of Canada through the Canada Book Fund (CBF) and the Canada Council for the Arts, and the Province of British Columbia through the British Columbia Arts Council and the Book Publishing Tax Credit.

20 19 18   3 4 5

Printed in Canada

To all my secret sources.
Right on.

Contents

Prologue

IT WAS THE MOST DRAMATIC *twist you could ever imagine in a murder trial. For four years, a killer had evaded the police. Even after being arrested he declared his innocence and fought for his freedom. But he was convicted of first-degree murder and sentenced to life imprisonment with no parole for 25 years. Still insisting he didn't do it, he successfully appealed the conviction. The appeal court judges agreed with his lawyers that a legal technicality had played out against him. The conviction was quashed, and he earned a new trial.*

This time, as the retrial got under way in 1995, the legal technicalities seemed to be working in the prisoner's favour. Testimony from one witness against him was struck down by the judge and could not be admitted as evidence. John

Antinello was winning the fight against the charge that he had murdered Sherwin Fettig. Antinello was edging ever closer to freedom.

Suddenly, Antinello's lawyer stopped the proceedings right in the middle of the prosecution's case. When the trial resumed, Antinello dropped a bombshell. He confessed to the killing and pleaded guilty to second-degree murder, knowing his plea brought with it the mandatory sentence of life in prison.

What brought about this sensational change of heart?

1

The Scree
Slope Skulls

A NEAT ROUND HOLE IN the skull, too large for any bullet, turned the case from a mystery to a murder. The crime came to light in one of the most spectacular surroundings imaginable, with the snow-capped Rocky Mountains towering in the background. From a high rocky precipice, a scree slope plunged at a dizzying angle down to the mirror-calm waters of Spray Lakes. And there, at the foot of the slope, lay a skull.

RCMP officers had feared human remains might be somewhere in the vicinity, hence the search, but never for a moment did they expect to find a skull with a neat hole in it. It was time for the forensic pathologists at the medical examiner's office to extract every possible secret from the skull. Whatever they found, it was clear this breathtaking stretch of Rocky Mountain scenery had just become the heart of a puzzling crime scene.

This scenic valley in Kananaskis Country, located beside one of its most picturesque lakes, had been a much happier place four years earlier. In July 1986, a special group of kids were taken there for a summer camp. These kids didn't often have such excitement. They were dubbed problem kids. Some were known runaways, and all of them were in the care of Alberta Social Services. The department had entrusted them to Ad Infinitum Treatment Services, an organization for troubled teens that was running the summer camp.

The remote forestry camp was accessible only by one rough gravel road and was isolated from the outside world with no telephones or radiotelephones. Towards the end of July, four staff members organized a wilderness camping trip, taking some of the kids into an even more remote section of the forest to set up a small campsite close to the lake.

During the first few days after arriving in the main camp, 13-year-old Billy Stuppard and 17-year-old Joey Platner struck up a close friendship and were among the group taken on the wilderness camping trip. They'd only been in this isolated spot for two days when on July 30, 1986, Billy, Joey and a third boy all decided to run away. Before nightfall, the third boy returned to the main camp, leaving Billy and Joey alone in the forest.

The group's small wilderness campsite had been set up not far from a lone camper called Richard Richards, who'd already been camping near the lake for some time, but was in no way connected to them. He was away exploring in the forest the night Billy and Joey ran away, and the two boys soon came across his empty tent and campsite.

None of the staff searched for the two missing boys, but the next day one of the childcare workers saw the two runaways in the group's canoe on the lake. One of the boys held aloft a crossbow and shouted obscenities before paddling off across the lake. At this point, the staff acted. They sent a message to the RCMP saying a canoe had capsized in the lake and two boys were missing.

Kananaskis RCMP constable Jim Kruk quickly contacted the nearest park ranger and ordered him to get a boat search under way. Kruk then raced to the lake and went out himself in a second boat. The two officers found nothing, so Constable Kruk called in a helicopter. Within 15 minutes of arriving on the scene, the helicopter crew spotted the canoe. It had apparently landed safely on the shore of the lake two kilometres away from the group's main camp. Once again, Kruk crossed the lake in his boat, and this time he found the canoe, which had been hidden in high weeds. It was upright and dry inside, with its paddles lying in the bottom. It was clear to Kruk that the two boys hadn't come to grief in the lake, but had landed and probably run away. Now the constable called in a dog handler and his sniffer dog from Banff National Park. They mounted a ground search north and south of the canoe, but despite working into the evening they found nothing.

While Kruk was scouring the area, Richards, the man in the nearby tent, stopped him to report that his crossbow had been stolen from the campsite while he was away. The next day Richards travelled into Calgary and went to the office of Ad Infinitum Treatment Services to complain about his crossbow being stolen.

Meanwhile, the RCMP began a separate investigation into the theft. Numerous RCMP officers and park rangers resumed the search through the forest, assisted by the helicopter, but still found no trace of the two boys. Inquiries among the staff and kids at the group camp revealed that Billy and Joey had talked about running away to Vancouver, where they wanted to visit Expo '86. Police recalled that when they found the canoe they saw tracks leading off towards a gravel path, one that could have given access to roads leading to Vancouver. Believing the boys had hitchhiked out of Kananaskis Country and were on their way to Expo '86, the RCMP called off the search. For the first time, the boys' parents were notified that their sons were missing, but the strange disappearances were never made public.

Joey's parents, Virginia and Harris Platner, were angry that the search had been called off so soon simply because searchers thought the boys had run off to Vancouver. The RCMP argued that nothing more could be accomplished by continuing to search. After all, their helicopter and ground-search teams had scoured the area thoroughly.

Billy's dad, Brian Stuppard, was angry that he hadn't

been told immediately that his son was missing. Brian decided to search for his son in Vancouver. He thought Billy might try to contact his grandfather, who lived there, and immediately warned Grandpa to keep a watchful eye open for the boy. Meanwhile, Brian kept on searching for Billy, not only in Vancouver, but also in other major cities. After all, it wasn't implausible that Billy had run away. He had become difficult to handle and was a regular runaway after the death of his mother in 1982, when he was nine years old. Further, Billy lost his grandmother and grandfather in quick succession soon afterwards. "His way of dealing with problems was just to run away," said Brian.

Over the next two years, Brian contacted police departments in several provinces. Finally, he turned to missing children's organizations and called on the Salvation Army. "I made it my business to search for him everywhere. I hunted all over western Canada," said Brian. Ever hopeful, he sought his son all through 1987 and 1988.

Sadly, on May 16, 1989, nearly three years after the boys disappeared, hikers found a skull only a couple of kilometres from where the group campsite had been set up. It was sent to the medical examiner's office in Calgary, where a forensic pathologist determined it was Joey Platner.

RCMP officers went back to the site and discovered a few more human bones and some items of clothing before a heavy snowfall forced them to abandon their search. Though they'd found Joey's remains, police had no definite evidence to say what had happened to Billy. Kananaskis RCMP staff sergeant Keith MacMillan told the media he wasn't very optimistic that the second boy would be found alive.

Brian received the news stoically. "I'm keeping my chin up," he said, "One has to be optimistic, but logic tells me there's not much hope."

Joey's parents planned a quiet funeral service for their son, who'd been a student at Shaughnessy Secondary School in Calgary. Police told his parents it simply looked like the boys had got lost. "There is no way of determining the cause of death at this point," said RCMP sergeant John Metcalfe. "At the time they went missing there was nothing to suggest foul play." Joey's mother, Virginia, said that from the bones the hikers had found it was evident that Joey had suffered a broken leg. The family had feared the worst during the three years Joey was missing, as they were certain he wouldn't go that long without contacting them.

From the little information Brian Stuppard had been given, he formed his own theory of what had happened. He knew the boys likely had a crossbow. Perhaps they had gone hunting in the woods, and there had been a fall or a rockslide that Joey hadn't survived. Maybe Billy hadn't survived either. It fit the known facts.

Two weeks after the discovery of the skull, on June 1, Brian's theory seemed to be proved right. As soon as the weather improved, the RCMP resumed their search of the area, and Brian was on the slopes with them when they discovered more clothing. The bloodstained jeans and other items of clothing finally destroyed Brian's hope that Billy was still alive. Located at the bottom of a slope, the clothing confirmed the speculation that they had fallen. "This kind of brings things pretty close to an end," said Brian. "It certainly appears as if they fell." As Joey had been confirmed dead and was in the care of Alberta Social Services at the time he died, the provincial attorney general's department ordered a routine fatality inquiry for October 1989 into his apparent accidental death.

Suddenly, a sensational twist changed everything. Mysteriously, the RCMP postponed the inquiry. All they would say was that they were investigating some startling new development. Inspector Bob Tramley now said foul play wasn't being ruled out. That meant Joey's death might be murder. For three months, the RCMP probed their new lead without revealing what it all meant. It seemed to revolve around some man who had since committed suicide, but by December the lead petered out. Tramley now said the investigators were no further ahead than they had been before, and a complete report on what they had discovered was passed on to the chief medical examiner's office.

All through the winter, deep snow and freezing temperatures prevented any more searches being carried out in Kananaskis Country, but once the snow had melted in early June 1990, RCMP and park rangers were back out on the scree slopes near the lake. On June 11, the final piece of the jigsaw puzzle fell into place. At the bottom of the scree slope they found the second skull, and to their amazement, it had a neat round hole in it. It was sent to the chief medical examiner's office in Calgary. Forensic pathologists confirmed that it was Billy Stuppard, and it no longer looked like he had died by accident. It looked like he'd been murdered and that this area was the crime scene.

This time there was no postponing the fatality inquiry. When it opened before Judge A.W. Aunger in Canmore in August 1990, it delivered one shock after another. First, the RCMP revealed all the latest information they had learned. They felt sure a man suffering from schizophrenia had murdered the two boys by shooting them with his crossbow or pushing them off the top of the scree slope. Later, he'd killed himself. It was Richard Richards.

Canmore RCMP corporal Al MacIntyre told the inquiry that police knew that Richards, a 27-year-old confirmed schizophrenic from Stony Plain, near Edmonton, was the man in the campsite next to the group camp where Billy and Joey were staying. He'd twice been treated for schizophrenia in the Misericordia Hospital in Edmonton, in 1984 and in early 1986. He'd reported that his tent had been broken into and his crossbow stolen. But police had no reason to believe he was connected with the disappearance of the two boys until after he committed suicide on March 13, 1987. Everything changed when police talked to one of Richards' associates.

Bernie Lehman said he'd been with Richards shortly

before he took his own life, and that Richards had acted in a bizarre manner. Lehman, put under hypnosis by investigators, revealed that Richards had showed him crude satanic drawings on the wall of an abandoned shed. They depicted a stick figure with a crossbow and the word "murder" written both forwards and backwards. Richards said there had been two guys who were evil, but that they would never do it again. He told Lehman he would burn in hell for what he had done to them. There would be no forgiveness. He had clearly been harbouring guilt for some time, as he had unsuccessfully tried to kill himself a few months earlier.

Putting all the evidence together, investigators knew for certain that Billy and Joey had broken into Richards' tent, stolen his crossbow and other valuables, and taken the canoe from the group camp. The two boys had spent some time in the nearby countryside shooting target practice with the crossbow. Investigators believed that some time later Richards, with his history of mental problems, became enraged at the thefts and had caught the two boys, marched them to the top of the perilous scree slope and then killed them.

Billy's father, who listened to all the evidence, knew exactly what it meant in his son's case. "There was a round hole in Billy's skull, too large for any bullet, which they [the police] believe was made by a crossbow bolt," he said. "That means, one way or another, that guy found the boys, disarmed them of the crossbow they'd stolen, and shot Billy through the head."

Police believe that having killed the boys, Richards probably pushed both bodies down the scree slope. It was likely this all happened soon after the search had been called off. The boys' bodies certainly weren't on the scree slope on the last day of the search, as the helicopter flew low over it several times and the crew saw nothing.

Shocking new facts emerged at the inquiry when the childcare workers from the group campsite testified. They now reluctantly revealed what they had known but kept secret at the time the boys disappeared. They suspected Richards had been a disruptive influence on the troubled kids at the camp, supplying them with liquor and maybe even drugs, and that he had even had sex with one of the girls. At one stage the staff went to the Spray Lakes park ranger and asked him to remove Richards because he was a pest. But they didn't tell the ranger what they believed had been going on regarding the booze, drugs and sex. Not knowing the serious nature of what he was dealing with, the ranger was powerless to remove the man.

One camp counsellor told the judge that after the two boys ran away he'd heard them rummaging through Richards' tent and campsite, but did nothing to stop them. What was worse, he didn't report to his superiors that he knew the boys were breaking the law by stealing from someone's campsite. Nor did the staff tell their superiors they knew some of the kids had committed other crimes during the camp.

By the time the fatality inquiry ended, everyone had a pretty clear picture of what had happened, but Judge Aunger officially listed the medical cause of death for each boy as "unascertainable." He listed the manner of death, which could include the possibilities of "natural, homicidal, suicidal, or accidental," as "undeterminable." He agreed that the RCMP's theory that Richards killed the two boys fit the established facts, but added that there was "nothing conclusive" upon which he could find a cause of death.

However, the judge had a lot to say about how badly this camp had been run. He stated that Alberta Social Services must ensure that future camps run by organizations on their behalf would be run in a way that prevented such a tragedy from being repeated. The judge came up with three recommendations: first, in future all childcare workers employed in group homes should get instruction in how to apply government regulations regarding childcare; second, all means of conveyance (which in this case had been a canoe) should be secured out of the reach of the kids; and third, any suspected crime should be immediately reported to the RCMP.

Judge Aunger blasted the camp staff for not telling anyone when they saw kids from their camp committing crimes, and for not passing on vital information about the two missing boys and Richards. He also commented, "The tenor of the childcare workers collectively was an attempt to blame the RCMP and park rangers. If those childcare workers had conveyed their knowledge and suspicions of crimes being committed to the proper authorities, those authorities would have had grounds upon which to act and check out any suspicious character."

The representative of the group running the camp defended her staff. Director Carol Freeman told the inquiry they could only "guarantee to do as much as is humanly possible" to control the children in their care.

Four years after the fatality inquiry, Billy's dad, Brian, made a major effort to use his son's death as a warning to other parents of kids in care to monitor closely the people looking after their children. Brian, who'd been a childcare worker years earlier, was angry and upset by the knowledge that his son's death could have been prevented. He believed that the staff at the camp had left his son out in the wild knowing he was in potential danger from a deranged man. "What bothers me most is that it should never have happened. People who knew enough to possibly prevent the tragedy, didn't tell," he said. "Instead of telling anyone, these people kept silent and the boys were left out there alone."

Ultimately, the deaths of Billy and Joey did bring some improvement to how troubled kids in care are looked after. Alberta Social Services say the deaths may have already indirectly saved other children's lives. The stinging rebuke from the judge at the fatality inquiry brought immediate action from Alberta Social Services in 1990. "We changed the regulations and toughened them up right away," said Bob Scott, the spokesman at the time. The new rules dictate a much closer look at which kids should be taken on such camping trips in the first place. As well, new regulations ensure that kids at camps are much more closely supervised.

Perhaps the last word should rest with Brian Stuppard. He tells parents that they shouldn't take it for granted that their kids are in good hands; they should check and satisfy themselves that they are. As Brian put it, "Remember Billy."

2

How Does
Your Garden Grow?

IT WAS ALL GOSSIP AND tittle-tattle. People said the old man at Number 662 had been done away with and his bones buried in his backyard. No one had any proof to take to the police, but in 1980 it was probably the best gossip in the whole of Medicine Hat.

Over the years since then, the old lady living at Number 662 had moved away to Pincher Creek, and new people had moved in. By then, the gossip had been elevated to persistent rumour. The old house was bought and sold a few times. Each new owner eventually came to hear the old rumour, but took no notice of it. The backyard had a vegetable patch and a profusion of flowers in the borders surrounding the fine lawn. One family even built a small playground for their children, with a little slide and a swing.

So it came as quite a shock when one day, 17 years after the gossip first started, something strange happened at Number 662. Quietly and without any fanfare or fuss, a few nondescript vehicles parked outside the neat little house, and a team of men moved in silently behind the high fence. They were police officers. When they'd finished digging, they had turned the infamous backyard, the source of decades of gossip and rumour, into a full-blown crime scene. They had found the bones the gossips always said were there.

Tadeus (Ted) Gawron and his wife, Sofia, had moved into Number 662 in the 1970s. They were a Polish couple who had met when they were both interned by the Nazis in a Polish concentration camp towards the end of the Second World War. In Medicine Hat they were known as a hard-working couple. Ted was a pensioner who had built a career working for Canadian Pacific Railway (CPR), and Sofia worked in a large greenhouse in the city. They had four children, two sons and two daughters, all of whom eventually moved away, leaving Ted and Sofia living in the house alone.

By 1980, things were not going well between Ted and Sofia. They were both 63, and Ted's health was seriously deteriorating. According to Sofia, they decided to separate in July and agreed on a division of their property. There was no divorce. Ted took his share in cash and was no longer seen at Number 662. Sofia said Ted had agreed that all his pension cheques should keep coming to the house, and that he was happy for her to continue cashing them.

It seemed like a perfectly ordinary separation, one repeated hundreds of times in every city. Couples find they can't live together any longer; one of the partners moves out, and the other stays in the house. After some time, Sofia tired of living at Number 662 on her own and decided to move west to Pincher Creek, where she would be nearer some of her children. She had a giant "moving-house" garage sale, sold the house and moved away. She settled into a quiet, solitary life in Pincher Creek and seldom spoke of her husband, who she said had left her.

Sofia wasn't talking much about Ted, but back in Medicine Hat everybody else was. People didn't buy the story about old Ted simply leaving home as part of a separation. They said he'd disappeared, vanished off the face of the earth. More precisely, he'd disappeared under the face of the earth, said the wagging tongues, buried in the backyard of Number 662.

There was plenty of fuel for the gossip. Shortly after Ted disappeared, neighbours noticed that Sofia had a high fence built around the yard. They could hardly help noticing it, as it was reckoned to be the highest fence in Medicine Hat. It was built of six-foot slab boards and was topped with barbed wire. "She put braces up to support it with two rows of barbed wire," said one neighbour. "It was like the Berlin Wall." All the neighbours asked themselves the same question: "Whatever could a person be doing in their backyard that would warrant such a barrier to keep out prying eyes?"

They couldn't see what was happening inside the yard, but they could see what was coming over the barbed wire. Thick, foul-smelling smoke rose over the fence for several days. It was obvious something substantial and stomach turning was being burned in an old barrel behind the fence. And what was the significance of all that topsoil? One evening around this time, a great mound of topsoil was delivered and dumped into the driveway of Number 662. Sofia made numerous back-and-forth trips with her wheelbarrow, moving the whole lot into the backyard.

As the gossip flourished, passing remarks from Sofia assumed major importance, and people convinced themselves more and more that old Ted had been done away with. One elderly neighbour in her eighties remembered a most illuminating conversation she had with Sofia shortly after Ted had "left home." For the previous two years, Ted, known to all as a helpful and hard-working man, had rototilled this neighbour's garden, as it was too much for her to handle. Not knowing the Gawrons had split up, the neighbour went to the house to ask Ted if he could tackle her garden again that year.

Sofia told her he had left, and naturally the neighbour asked her when he'd be back. "He's never coming home," said Sofia. Soon, these words of Sofia were to be firmly embedded in the gossip. For the rumour mongers, Sofia's sure knowledge that old Ted wouldn't be coming home had nothing to do with him having left her. Everyone reckoned they knew the real reason. The clincher was Sofia's huge garage sale. The neighbours noticed that Sofia was selling all of old Ted's most prized possessions: his gardening tools, bicycle and fishing gear. If he had left her, as Sofia claimed, he would have taken all those items with him, said the gossips. No, she was selling them off because she knew he had no more need of them.

Although these rumours were rampant in the neighbourhood, not a word reached the ears of the police. It was one thing to gossip and whisper about such ghastly suspicions over a cup of coffee in the privacy of your own kitchen, but it would be too awful to voice these outrageous and scandalous accusations out loud. So, eventually, the neighbourhood around Number 662 settled back into its normal routine. The scuttlebutt only resurfaced on the occasions when the house was sold and new occupiers arrived. When one family moved in, they employed a professional landscaper to redesign the backyard for them. They'd heard the rumour and mentioned it in passing to their gardener, telling him to watch out for human bones in the yard. He didn't find any.

While Ted and Sofia's children understood their parents had separated, they grew concerned over the years that none of them had heard a word from their father. They knew he was still alive. After all, their mother was still cashing his pension cheques regularly. One day, the couple's son Kenneth, who hadn't had any personal contact with Ted since 1980, checked more carefully with his two sisters and his brother. Only then did the realization hit home that none of them had actually heard from Ted in the past seven years.

In 1987, Kenneth went to Medicine Hat city police and reported his father as a missing person. As soon as the Canada Pension Plan authorities were informed that Ted was officially listed as missing and hadn't physically cashed his own pension cheques for the past seven years, alarm bells started ringing. They contacted Sofia telling her she had no legal right to be cashing the cheques. She stopped doing it. The CPR police also opened an investigation into where Ted Gawron's company pension had been going.

Kenneth and the rest of the family spent the next four years trying to track down where Ted had gone. One neighbour, a truck driver who knew him back in 1980 before he disappeared, said Ted had talked about perhaps becoming a trucker. But he obviously never did. Kenneth checked everywhere. The various pension offices had no records of him for the past decade. The family contacted every known friend and every contact at CPR, but no one had seen him since 1980. Police missing persons inquiries across Canada turned up no trace.

Finally, in 1991, after Ted had been missing for more than 10 years and his children had searched for him everywhere for four years, Kenneth applied to have his father legally presumed dead. On November 5, 1991, a judge in the Court of Queen's Bench at Lethbridge made it official. He declared Ted was no longer just missing—he was dead.

Another six years passed. Only a few old-timers still lived in the same neighbourhood that Ted and Sofia had left all those years before. Some of their original neighbours had moved, and others had passed away. Their old house had changed hands a few times over the years, and those presently living there had never heard of them.

By 1997, the old neighbourhood was modernizing as it approached the 21st century. Several new families moving into the street had their yards converted, adding swimming pools and even a Jacuzzi or two. So when a few vehicles pulled up outside Number 662 in May 1997, and a group of workmen went through into the backyard carrying heavy tools, neighbours assumed it was just another swimming pool in the making. The men worked in overalls and jeans, like any other crew of workmen, and turned up every day for nearly a week, about the average time it takes to build a swimming pool. Then they left.

But they weren't workmen at all. They were police officers and crime scene investigators on an undercover operation, and when they dug up the backyard of Number 662, they found human bones. Because it was a suspected crime scene, the police had been keeping it all under wraps. At the time, it was the most closely guarded secret in Medicine Hat. Their covert investigation had begun five months earlier in January 1997. City police decided to look again at the Ted Gawron missing persons file, which had been unsolved for 17 years. Lead investigator Sergeant Mick Nieman and his partner, Sergeant Andy McGrogan, had started by interviewing anyone who knew Ted nearly two decades previously. They swore everyone they interviewed to silence, to protect their undercover operation.

After months of inquiries, they were pretty sure that digging up the backyard of Number 662 was the only way to solve the disappearance. But they still wanted secrecy, hence the few "workmen" in nondescript vehicles who arrived in the street without a police car or police uniform in sight. Not a word got out about what they'd been doing, and no one knew what they'd found. The human remains were sent to the medical examiner's office in Calgary, where it was some time before forensic pathologists there were finally able to determine that the bones were all that remained of Ted Gawron.

Still, no one in Medicine Hat was any the wiser. Even the media had no suspicion of the drama that had played out unseen at Number 662. The veil of secrecy drawn over the affair had been a total success. That is, until someone sworn to silence could stand it no longer. Amazingly, the story didn't break in Medicine Hat at all, but 400 kilometres away at the *Calgary Sun*, where a certain crime reporter had heard a whisper. He did his own digging and came up with an exclusive three-page scoop, revealing all.

On the day his newspaper story hit the streets, Medicine Hat police called a press conference and confirmed that officers had discovered Ted Gawron's remains, chopped into pieces and buried in his own backyard. The gossips had hit the nail on the head 17 years ago. They were dead right all along.

Detectives hadn't yet been able to determine how Ted had died or who had dissected and scattered him, and a full-blown criminal investigation was still underway, they said. Very soon police let it be known publicly that none of the four Gawron children was suspected of having any involvement in his death. Each had been completely eliminated as a suspect. But investigators weren't making any comment either way about Sofia. Staff Sergeant Lou O'Reilly of the Medicine Hat police said no one had been arrested and no charges had been laid. He predicted it would be a lengthy investigation.

As the story was breaking, Sofia was where she had been for the past few years, in the long-term-care ward of the Crowsnest Pass Health Care Centre in Blairmore in the Rocky Mountains. Staff members were careful to let no one speak with Sofia, and wouldn't talk about her. It was known that the facility was home to some of the most seriously ill seniors in southern Alberta, many suffering advanced Alzheimer's disease and other forms of dementia. Most required round-the-clock care and supervision. But, said the facility's administrator, Pat Rypien, just because Sofia had been there for a number of years no one should assume she was confused or incompetent.

A dramatic breakthrough came in August 1997. Crime scene investigators thought they'd finally solved the mystery of how Ted Gawron had died. They discovered poison in the soil that had been kept as evidence from around the dismembered skeleton at the crime scene. Crown Prosecutor Darwin Greaves said it was a major find. It was thought to be an insecticide widely used in industrial greenhouses 15 to 20 years previously, at the time Ted Gawron died. It was now known to be so toxic that it had since been banned. Greaves pointed out that Medicine Hat was the greenhouse capital of the world, a comment that wasn't lost on those who remembered Sofia had worked for years in one of the city's industrial greenhouses.

No Alberta crime laboratory had the facilities to positively identify the mysterious poison, so Greaves ordered police to send it to an independent laboratory, even in the United States if necessary, to get it identified. Whatever it was, it was frighteningly toxic. "It's the bad stuff. It would make you glow in the dark," he said.

Forensic pathologists studied the bones again to see if any showed signs of being contaminated by the poison. Greaves wanted to know if there was evidence the poison had been the instrument of death for Ted. The answer came in October. Medicine Hat police travelled to Sofia's bedside in the Blairmore nursing home on October 9 to charge the 80-year-old widow in connection with her husband's death and with fraud over the pension cheques. It was immediately clear that they hadn't found any evidence that poison had killed old Ted, and there was no evidence that Sofia had any hand in actually killing him. She was charged with "offering an indignity to a human body by dissecting and concealing it." It meant police were confident that after 17 years they probably had strong enough evidence to secure a conviction if the case went to trial. They believed they could prove that Sofia had dismembered her husband and buried the pieces in various parts of her backyard.

Sofia was also charged with fraud over $5,000 for claiming Ted's CPR pension after he was dead. She faced a similar charge for claiming Ted's Canada Pension Plan money after his demise, and a third fraud charge for claiming his Old Age Security money.

Medicine Hat Crown prosecutor Stephanie Cleary pointed out that no murder charge had been laid against Sofia as no cause of death had been established. The police allegation was that one way or another Ted Gawron had died. He was known to be extremely ill and may have died of natural causes, or it was possible some unknown person may have given him poison. But whatever had happened, Sofia had been faced with his death. Police were alleging that even if she had done nothing wrong prior to his death, what she did next was criminal. Instead of revealing his demise, which would cause his pensions to end, she chose to dismember and bury him and pretend to the world that he had left her and was still alive. His pensions would continue to roll in, and she could live off them. Police were alleging that their evidence showed this ruse was successful for at least seven years. This was why the body concealment and fraud charges were linked.

At a press conference, the police took the unusual step of thanking the neighbourhood around Number 662 for its part in the marvellous conspiracy of silence it maintained during the investigation. Staff Sergeant O'Reilly praised all the residents in the neighbourhood for keeping everything confidential. "Their tight lips and co-operation" greatly assisted the investigators as they made discreet inquiries at a critical stage, he said.

O'Reilly also singled out the current residents of Number 662 for their "total co-operation, patience, and understanding for all the inconvenience" caused by having police almost living in their house and backyard.

The occupiers of Number 662, Patsy Walker and her family, eventually did speak to reporters. She said the family had never felt uncomfortable that bones were found in their backyard. "The only thing that has ever haunted us is the media," she said. After the story broke, the house became an object of fascination for reporters and voyeurs who repeatedly drove past it. "I feel very sorry for the Gawron family, but we've just been bystanders," said Patsy.

In late January 1998, Sofia, who was then 81 years old and confined to a wheelchair, was wheeled into a Medicine Hat courtroom by her two daughters for the legal proceedings. In question was Sofia's mental fitness to stand trial. Legal and psychiatric experts agreed she didn't know what was going on around her and was unfit to go through a trial. Crown Prosecutor Cleary presented a vital report by Dr. Kenneth Hashman, the clinical director of the forensic unit at the Peter Lougheed Centre in Calgary. Legally, his report meant Sofia didn't understand what was being alleged against her, didn't know how to instruct her own lawyer and had no idea of what could happen to her as the outcome of a trial.

The judge accepted the report and on January 22, 1998, he declared Sofia unfit to stand trial. It meant she was unlikely ever to do so, as there was little likelihood her mental powers would improve in time. He ordered that she should continue living at the Blairmore hospital. He said he was satisfied the public was adequately protected by her being in there, and she didn't pose any risk to anyone. Some people questioned why the law had gone after Sofia at all after 17 years. Cleary spelled it out very simply. "This is to demonstrate that justice will catch up with you, no matter how much time passes and no matter where you go," she said.

As for all the gossips in Medicine Hat who could say, "I told you so" when Ted's remains were found, one person summed it all up more accurately than any other. One of Sofia's neighbours was an author. When the rumours were at their height, years before Ted's bones were discovered, this neighbour was attending university. For her contribution to a short-story writing course, she penned a fictional story based loosely on local gossip. Only when Ted's remains were discovered in his backyard, years later, did she realize how aptly she had titled her work. It was called "And How Does Your Garden Grow?"

3

That Sinking Feeling

PEOPLE PARK PICKUP TRUCKS ILLEGALLY in Calgary's streets every day, and police haul the vehicles down to the impound lot in droves. Among the vehicles towed on April 4, 1991, was a white truck. Some inconsiderate jerk had parked it in an alley completely blocking a resident's driveway. No owner came to claim it at the lot, so police looked inside for keys. They didn't find any. They did find, however, that the cab was heavily splashed with blood and that the window had been smashed in. Suddenly, a truck in a routine parking violation became an instant crime scene, and if investigators weren't mistaken—with all that blood—the crime was murder.

Detectives quickly formed a shrewd idea of who was at the centre of the mystery. Three days before the white Ford

Super Cab truck turned up, its usual driver, Sherwin Aaron Fettig, a 23-year-old butcher with Canada Safeway, had been reported missing. Sherwin used to live in Medicine Hat and had moved to Calgary three years earlier to study at the Southern Alberta Institute of Technology (SAIT), after which he'd taken the job at Safeway. Every Sunday he telephoned his dad, Tony, in Medicine Hat. It was Tony's truck, but Sherwin was using it. Apparently, Sherwin was in good spirits when he made his regular Sunday call to his dad. It was the day before April Fools' Day, and Sherwin was cracking jokes about helping to stack Easter eggs. The next day he disappeared. "He was cheerful and happy. We don't know what's going on or why he should disappear," Tony told the media.

Investigators released photographs of Sherwin, who had a distinctive black moustache, and of his white truck with its custom-built bumper and bed laden with straw. Whatever police found in the cab of the truck led them to take Sherwin's disappearance very seriously. He wasn't just a missing person—homicide detectives had released the pictures, and it was clearly their case. There appeared to be two possible scenarios. Did someone kill Sherwin in the truck and then dispose of him? Or was Sherwin the killer who'd murdered someone in the truck and now gone on the run?

Homicide detectives theorized that the violent world of drug dealing might be involved, because in 1987 Sherwin had been handed a three-year prison stretch for trafficking in cocaine. Medicine Hat cops knew he'd been busy on the drug scene across southern Alberta for years.

Crime scene investigators sent the blood and smashed glass from inside the cab to the RCMP crime laboratory in Edmonton for testing. The initial tests didn't answer the big question. Months passed while new tests were carried out, but finally, six months after Sherwin disappeared, homicide detectives had their answer. Laboratory DNA analysis proved the blood in the cab was from Sherwin. He was the murder victim, not the killer. In October 1991, the day after this was announced, his father made an emotional public plea. He urged anyone who knew what had happened to his son to come forward with information. Even if detectives were certain he was dead, the family still had no body to bury.

The appeal fell on deaf ears, and homicide detectives knew why. They were tracking Sherwin's last known movements through the murky underworld of drug dealings with all its threats, rip-offs and violence. No hard-faced drug trafficker in this scene would be helping police with information or listening to emotional pleas from family members.

For six more months the veil of secrecy over Sherwin's murder held, but in April 1992 homicide detectives got a vital breakthrough. An underworld informant told an officer he should be talking to a certain woman who used to be the girlfriend of a major drug dealer in the city. Bonnie would have a lot to tell them, he said. Investigators tracked

Bonnie down, and she was as good as the informant's word. She knew where Sherwin's body was, she said. If they'd take her up in a police aircraft she could point out the very spot where he was buried in a shallow grave in a remote area west of the city. When they were northwest of Cochrane, Bonnie pointed down to a lonely acreage and pinpointed the exact place where they should dig.

The cops were confident. On April 15, 1992, in a rare move, Inspector Ray McBrien, who was in charge of the major crimes section, invited the media on a trip into the countryside. Reporters and photographers gathered at the acreage where McBrien had set up his command post, and the ground search for a body began. A team of 18 men including city homicide detectives, the TAC-Team, the K-9 dog handlers and Cochrane RCMP officers were photographed searching through the acreage before they started digging at the pinpointed spot.

A skeleton was found exactly where Bonnie said it would be. It was wrapped in a sleeping bag embedded with fragments of glass from a vehicle window. The acreage was now a crime scene and was cordoned off with yellow police tape. Thanks to the media being right on hand, the discovery was immediately publicized. Finding Sherwin Fettig's remains after all this time was major news. The headlines were exactly what homicide detectives wanted, and they had engineered it that way. During all this time, undercover cops had a suspect under surveillance, and were waiting hopefully for a guilty reaction on his part the moment the news broke.

That evening, forensic pathologists in the Calgary medical examiner's office confirmed through dental records that the skeleton was all that remained of Sherwin Fettig. He had been shot in the head.

It was no accident that the secret informant produced the vital breakthrough when he did. Homicide detectives had spent a year putting Sherwin's background and that of the people around him under the microscope. The cops were confident they knew how he had been murdered and even why. When Bonnie led them to Sherwin's body, it was the last piece of the puzzle. Six days later they went out and arrested their suspect, Bonnie's one-time boyfriend, John Joseph Antinello, a 26-year-old convicted drug dealer. They charged him with first-degree murder.

When the case came to trial nearly 18 months later in September 1993, the jury at Calgary's Court of Queen's Bench was introduced to the dangerous world of drug dealing. Prosecutors revealed the full story, one that had taken homicide detectives a year to piece together. It sounded very simple. Sherwin had ripped Antinello off over a single small bag of cocaine worth $300, so Antinello shot him dead.

Crown Prosecutor Harold Hagglund outlined to jury members the amazing story of how Antinello almost pulled off the perfect crime. He had killed his victim and transported the body to a remote spot using the dead man's truck. He had buried the body in a shallow grave, and no one had seen him. There was no witness to link him to the scene. Incredibly, Antinello had even improved on perfection by constructing an airtight and unshakeable alibi. That very evening he had a scheduled appointment with his parole officer. All he had to do was get back to Calgary and arrive on time. In the future, if anyone accused him of being out in the foothills northwest of Cochrane burying anyone, he could truthfully say he was in Calgary with his parole officer.

It would be a race to get to the parole officer on time. Antinello turned Sherwin's white Ford Super Cab out of the acreage. In his panic, as he sped along a muddy track, the wheels slithered into deep mud and bogged down. Now what could he do? If he didn't get help he would be late and miss the vital appointment with the parole officer. He had no option. Very literally, he had a sinking feeling things were about to go wrong. He went to the neighbouring acreage and fetched the owner to help pull him out of the mud.

His perfect murder plan was suddenly in tatters. Antinello was driving a murdered man's truck on the only track leading away from the acreage where one day the body would be found. And now a witness could put him there. One final detail completed the disaster. As Antinello stood in the thick mud pushing Sherwin's truck while the helpful neighbour steered, the truck lurched. The gun Antinello had used slid out from under the passenger seat and the witness saw it.

Prosecutor Hagglund made sure the neighbour, the vital witness, was one of the first people to testify to the jury. The one-time biker remembered the white Ford Super Cab stuck in the mud, and he remembered it was in April 1991. He remembered the gun, which he kicked back under the seat, and he remembered who was driving the truck.

The difficulty prosecutors now faced was getting other witnesses to testify on the stand. In the drug world no one dares rat on a drug dealer, especially not on a man already accused of executing someone who crossed him. Added to that, the prosecution would be relying on the testimony of witnesses from inside the drug world, some of them convicted criminals. Would a jury believe them?

One man knew enough to put Antinello away for life, and Hagglund put him on the stand right away. Mr. X refused to testify. The judge warned him he would be in contempt of court and spelled out the man's choices. Either the reluctant witness would testify or the judge would jail him for 90 days. The man saw his choices in a different light. Either he would testify—and Antinello would do his worst—or he could remain silent and the judge would do his worst. Mr. X feared Antinello more. He defied the judge and did his 90 days in jail, which he served keeping his mouth shut the whole time.

The prosecution had better luck with Bonnie, Antinello's former girlfriend who had led police to Sherwin's body in the first place. She told the jury that one day in 1991 while he was high on cocaine, Antinello had talked to her about a missing person called Sherwin Fettig. Antinello told her that he and Sherwin had gone together to meet a new drug dealer. Sherwin had made some smart remark that irked the dealer. The drug dealer had promptly shot him twice in the head. Antinello said the dealer had forced him to dispose of the body, or he'd get shot as well.

At the time when Antinello was confessing to his girlfriend he had buried Sherwin northwest of Cochrane, everyone else thought Sherwin was just a missing person. Antinello was saying he knew Sherwin was dead months before the body was found, though he wasn't the murderer. This became Antinello's defence. His lawyer argued that, no matter what any other witnesses might say, all Antinello did was bury Sherwin's body after someone else killed him.

But after the body was found exactly where Antinello told his girlfriend he'd buried it, he did a lot more talking, and this time he was telling a different story. In talking with fellow drug dealers, he confessed to being the shooter as well. A drug dealer, who was allowed to keep his identity secret, testified that as soon as Sherwin's body was found, Antinello told him he had to leave town in a hurry. Antinello said Sherwin was a drug dealer who'd been ripping off customers. The witness said it was a shame Sherwin hadn't been able to pay him back his cash, to which Antinello replied, "I would have killed him even if he did pay me back."

After he was arrested, Antinello confessed to fellow

inmates that he'd murdered Sherwin. At least, that's what the jailbird witnesses told the jury. The question was whether or not the jury would believe them. Antinello's defence lawyers made sure the jury knew these men had earned sweet deals from the police in return for their testimony. One inmate who'd shared a cell with Antinello in the Calgary Remand Centre told the jury that Antinello said he'd killed Sherwin after being ripped off for "an eight-ball of coke," no more than $300 worth of cocaine. "That's why John popped him," he said.

John had thoughts of "popping" some other people, as well. He was angry with Bonnie for leading police to Sherwin's body and wanted to put out a hit on her, said the witness. This witness had mentioned to John that he was having serious problems with one of his own enemies in the drug world. "John told me he could arrange to have done to that guy the same thing he'd done to Fettig—pop him," said the witness.

By the time the jury members retired to consider their verdict it all boiled down to whether or not they'd believe the stories told by these unsavoury characters paraded before them. What weight would they put on the evidence of convicted drug dealers who claimed that Antinello had confessed he was the shooter and had buried Sherwin's body?

They believed them. Just because they were drug dealers didn't mean they couldn't tell the truth when they had to. They found Antinello guilty of first-degree murder. On

October 2, 1993, Justice Allen Sulatycky sentenced Antinello to life in prison with no chance of parole for 25 years.

But Antinello wasn't done yet. His lawyers found a legal loophole that they claimed had tainted the evidence in the trial. They said one of the confessions Antinello had made to a jailbird should never have been allowed into evidence. To overcome the difficulty of getting this jailed drug dealer to give evidence, police had got drugs to him inside the jail. Alberta's Court of Appeal agreed with the lawyers that this was wrong. Antinello's appeal was upheld and a new trial started in November 1995.

This time the new judge, Justice Patrick Sullivan, wasn't going to make the same mistake. The first thing he did was throw out Antinello's confession to the jailed drug dealer. It was "not moral or lawful" for police to smuggle drugs into a prison to get a witness to talk, he said. But that still left two other witnesses who maintained Antinello had confessed to them that he'd shot Sherwin Fettig dead and buried him.

Suddenly, a dramatic twist ended the trial. Antinello talked with his lawyer. There was an adjournment, and when the court reconvened, Antinello confessed to everyone that he was the killer. He pleaded guilty to second-degree murder. Antinello said that he'd shot Sherwin dead, though he disputed the amount of drugs in the rip-off deal. He claimed that he wouldn't have killed Sherwin for ripping him off for $300 worth of coke—he did it because Sherwin had ripped him off for drugs worth $2,000.

Why did Antinello have such a dramatic change of heart? It all centred on a decision by the judge to allow a police-videotaped interview into evidence. You may recall that Mr. X had been a vital witness whose testimony would have been the clincher against Antinello at his first trial. But, being scared of what Antinello might do to him, he never testified about what he knew.

Police, however, had his vital evidence on a videotaped interview. Calgary homicide detective Allan Hargreaves, who carried out the questioning, would never forget that crucial interview. On the day police found Mr. X, they knew that Hargreaves, the lead investigator who had led the digging for Fettig's body at the crime scene, must interview the vital witness.

There was a problem. When he took the telephone call saying Mr. X was in police hands, Hargreaves wasn't at work. He was at home on his sickbed with a serious attack of influenza, almost unable to move. Years of work on the case depended on this interrogation, so Hargreaves dragged himself into the office and interviewed the man on videotape.

There was one vital point when considering whether or not the tape would be admissible as evidence. Had the testimony been forced out of Mr. X under duress? Had he been bullied into making his statement? Had any legal technicalities been infringed during the interview? When the video was shown no one could deny that Hargreaves had been dreadfully ill. At one point Mr. X even offered him a glass of water! It was immediately obvious that Hargreaves had been in no shape to exert any pressure at all on the witness. The video would be allowed into evidence.

On the tape, Mr. X explained how Antinello, the killer, had given him the task of cleaning up the blood in the victim's truck and disposing of the truck so it would never be found. But misfortune struck before Mr. X completed his task. After he'd cleaned off all the blood he could see, he was on his way to dispose of the truck when it suddenly broke down. The engine failure meant the failure of his mission. The truck wouldn't start, and he'd abandoned it in a back alley across a resident's driveway.

When Antinello knew the damning video was about to be used against him, he knew it would put him behind bars for 25 years. That's when he and his lawyers stopped the trial and engineered a deal. It wasn't a bad move by Antinello, who was 30 years old at the time. If he'd been convicted again of first-degree murder, he'd have to serve 25 years before even being considered for parole. By pleading guilty to second-degree murder, his parole eligibility was cut to 10 years, effectively giving him a chance to get out of prison 15 years earlier.

When the case was finished, a chilling observation came from Charlie Allard, whose acreage northwest of Cochrane was almost next door to where Sherwin's body was found. Sherwin was the third skeleton in seven months that had been dug up by police in shallow graves in the general area around Allard's acreage. The other two—a waitress and a teenaged girl, both from Calgary—were in no way connected to Sherwin Fettig. Their murders are still unsolved.

"This used to be a peaceful place," said Charlie Allard. "Now it seems to be a dumping ground for bodies."

4

Septic Tank Sam

IF EDMONTON-AREA FARMER Charlie McLeod hadn't been so frugal, the most baffling murder case in Alberta's history would never have been uncovered. On April 13, 1977, Charlie was installing a septic tank at the new farmhouse he was building on his property near Tofield outside Edmonton. All he needed was a pump to service it. He could have driven into town and bought a new one for a few dollars, but why spend money when he knew where there was a perfectly good working pump on his own property. An old abandoned farmhouse stood derelict not far away. It had a septic tank with a pump that was working fine, except no one had touched it since the place fell into disuse two years earlier. Charlie went to fetch the pump.

He got as far as taking the cover off the old, two-metre-deep waste tank. The first thing he saw was a dark grey woollen sock, which he pulled out, and then a shoe. That was enough for him. He grabbed them both and raced off to the RCMP detachment at Tofield, about 60 kilometres southeast of Edmonton. Someone was headfirst down his septic tank and the Mounties had better come quickly, he told them. They did. Corporal Ed Lammerts, in charge of the Tofield detachment at the time, and another officer followed Charlie back to the scene. For the next hour, the two Mounties scooped a foul-smelling, oozy liquid out of the tank with an ice cream pail until they finally discovered human remains. At first it was impossible to tell if it was a man or a woman. Whoever dumped the body in the tank had tipped a mass of lime on top, hoping to speed up its decomposition. After six hours of careful work, the two officers, backed up by crime scene investigators, had removed the skeletal remains, which were then taken to the medical examiner's office in Edmonton.

Charlie's septic tank was now a major crime scene. He hadn't just discovered human remains—he had stumbled on one of the most horrific murders these officers had ever encountered. Though they had no idea who the victim was, forensic pathologists told them it was a man, and they knew exactly what he had endured. The remains and the tattered clothing clinging to them told a ghastly story.

First, he had been beaten and tied up. When he was

helpless to resist, his killers had tortured him mercilessly with a blowtorch, the burn marks still being visible on the remnants of his clothing. They had sexually mutilated him. When this probably hadn't killed him they shot him at least twice in the head and chest. Pathologists knew that at least two shots had been fired, as they found only two bones damaged by bullets. They didn't know if more than two shots had been fired, because bullets passing through a body without hitting bone leave no trace on a skeleton.

Corporal Lammerts didn't know who the man was, but he already had a mental picture of who his killers were. "They had to be cruel and vindictive," he said. "To impose that much pain on someone who was most likely alive is extremely bizarre. It's amazing what some people will do to other people."

He thought the killers probably knew the area well. They likely knew that the old farm, about 13 kilometres west of Tofield, was abandoned and derelict. For them, it was a fair bet no one would ever look into that old septic tank. Even if anyone had missed the guy, his body would never be found. He would remain a missing person forever, and they'd be clean away with the perfect murder. Detectives knew it was only the sheer coincidence of Charlie McLeod needing a septic pump that revealed the murder at all.

Edmonton RCMP homicide detectives led the hunt for the killers, backed by the Tofield and Vegreville Mounties. Forensic pathologists were able to tell them the victim had been in the tank for at least three or four months. This was bad news for the detectives. It meant the victim had already been missing that long without anyone coming forward inquiring about him. It suggested he had no close family or friends. Getting him identified was going to be a problem.

Tofield's 1,200 residents were in shock when the details were released. One neighbouring farmer, Johnny Wood, went straight out and checked all the septic tanks on his property. He was relieved to find nothing out of the ordinary in any of them. Locals quickly took the view that if the killers knew where old Charlie McLeod's disused septic tank was, the killers must be locals. Bill Chin, who owned the Diamond Restaurant in Tofield, wondered if they might even be among his regular customers. John Baergen, who managed the town's Co-op store, had the same fear that the killers could be shopping in his store every day.

More than a month after the discovery, the murder was still the talk of the town, and the *Tofield Mercury* ran a full-page feature under the headline: GRISLY MURDER CASE HAS RCMP BAFFLED. The list of major unknowns was daunting. The detectives had no idea who the victim was. They had no suspects. They knew of no motive for the crime. And there was no evidence to suggest the killing was carried out at the derelict farmhouse. The septic tank was just the dumpsite. That meant they had no idea where the main crime scene was. No one had missed the victim, and that could even mean he was a transient passing through the area.

Until they could identify him, it was a hopeless task. They had theories and speculations, any one of which could be on the mark or way off. Maybe this was a biker gang killing. Would outlaw biker gang members be capable of torturing a rival gangland member with a blowtorch, shooting him and making his body disappear? It was possible.

What about the sexual mutilation? Could the killer be a husband who had caught this man with his wife and wreaked a terrible revenge? That was possible as well. It might also explain why the killer had gone to such enormous lengths to make sure the victim could never be identified. If the victim were ever named, some confidant would be bound to know of his adulterous affair. That would reveal the name of the woman and lead to the murderous husband.

Was this a drug deal that went wrong? Was it a bad debt? Was the victim harbouring some secret that he gave up under torture before being executed? Was it a falling out among thieves? Was he tortured to reveal where his share of the spoils of some major crime were hidden? Did the victim fall into the hands of a sadistic murderer who tortured and killed him for pleasure? Any one of these theories could have been the answer.

The police decided to release a description of the victim, vague as it was. The most accurate details were the man's clothing. He had been wearing blue jeans, a blue Levi shirt with snap buttons, a white T-shirt, grey woollen work socks and imitation Wallabee shoes. Investigators tried to read his background from his clothing. He could have been a farm labourer or a construction worker. He could have come from a Native reserve. He could just as easily have been a homeless vagrant from the streets of Edmonton. They really couldn't narrow it down.

His physical description was even less definite than his clothing. He had black hair and was probably a Native, but may have been Caucasian. He was thought to be between 23 and 32 years old. Most newspaper reports went with an age between the two extremes, saying the victim was probably 28. He may have been 5 feet 10 inches (but could have been as short as 5 feet 6 inches or as tall as 6 feet), and he may have weighed 180 pounds (but could have weighed as little as 145 pounds). His bones and teeth revealed that he had suffered a serious illness when he was about five years old.

The publicity brought four potential leads. Investigators chased all four down and eliminated each one. Thorough checking of at least 250 missing persons files threw up no likely candidates. Two months after the discovery, in June 1977, investigators turned to Canada's dentists for help. First, they contacted all 800 dentists in Alberta, sending them the dental X-rays of the murder victim for comparison. He still had all his teeth, with some fillings and evidence of recent dental work. In case he'd arrived from out of province, they also contacted dental organizations in other provinces and placed notices in Canadian dental bulletins and magazines nationwide. They drew another complete blank.

Week after week the *Tofield Mercury* repeated the RCMP's plea for information about any missing person in the area, but eventually the case dropped out of the news. With no mourners present, the murder victim's remains were buried in an unmarked grave in an Edmonton cemetery.

Almost a year later the Tofield murder was handed over to Edmonton RCMP corporal Jamie Graham. In the homicide office he was given a file simply numbered "Unidentified Human Remains 77-001-38," which pretty well reflected how little it contained. However, Graham was enthusiastic and repeatedly succeeded in persuading the local media to run new features on the mystery. Each time, the publicity prompted new responses. Each time, new prospective leads were chased down. Every attempt failed to bring forth the answer. A couple of times, amazingly, the renewed publicity brought out characters who confessed to the killing, but it was easy for investigators to see through their stories and dismiss these hoaxers. At least Corporal Graham was achieving one of his aims—he was letting the killers know the murder investigation was still actively being pursued. "The chance of solving this one isn't all that good," he said, "but I don't want the person who did this ever to relax."

Early in 1979, a Calgary cop contacted Corporal Graham with an idea. He'd just read in a police gazette about a couple of American forensic scientists who could start with a skull and reconstruct an accurate likeness of the person's face. Perhaps they could at least put a face to the Tofield murder victim. It was exactly the boost Corporal Graham needed. He telephoned one of the scientists, Dr. Clyde Snow, a forensic anthropologist with the Federal Aviation Administration in Oklahoma, and explained his problem. Dr. Snow invited him to bring the skull and all the other bones with him, and they would rebuild the man's face. Dr. Snow had been working with Betty Gatliff, a medical illustrator with the Federal Aviation Administration, since 1967. Their success record was most impressive. At the time Corporal Graham contacted them, they had worked on more than 60 skulls and helped to produce positive identifications in more than two-thirds of their cases. This was remarkable when you considered that police and other agencies only consulted them when every other line of inquiry had been exhausted. Most of the cases were "no-hopers" long before Snow and Gatliff were brought into the picture.

Dr. Snow had become famous for working on an amazing case in the United States only three years earlier. In 1976, a television company was working on an episode of *The Six Million Dollar Man* in an old wooden funhouse called Laugh in the Dark at Long Beach, California. It was full of typical funhouse scary figures such as skeletons, wax dummies and ghosts. One wax figure, which was painted a glow-in-the-dark orange, was hanging from the ceiling on a make-believe gallows. It was in the film director's way, so he had it removed. As a film crew worker lifted it down, an arm fell off—

revealing a human bone. Dr. Snow was called in and was able to prove it was no dummy, but a mummified human corpse. Dr. Snow's brilliant work proved the remains were those of an infamous bank robber called Elmer J. McCurdy. A sheriff's posse had shot him dead in a barn at the turn of the century. His mummified remains became a freak-show attraction that went on for decades before Dr. Snow finally discovered where he'd ended up. As a result, Elmer J. McCurdy's remains were being given a decent burial in Guthrie, Oklahoma, in 1977— the same time Charlie McLeod was bringing the Tofield murder victim to light.

Corporal Graham had the Tofield remains exhumed, placed them in a box and flew to Oklahoma on a commercial airline with the box on his lap. He took the skull and bones to the Stovall Museum at the University of Oklahoma where he met Dr. Snow in his laboratory. Police officers had been bringing unidentified human remains to Dr. Snow since 1960. In the first seven years, the anthropologist had at least been able to tell police the sex, the approximate age, the race and the stature and physique of the remains. But in 1967 he teamed up with Betty Gatliff and together they had added facial reconstruction to their available expertise.

Dr. Snow got straight to work. He took about 50 measurements on the Tofield skull and 75 more on the various bones in the box. Then he ran all his numbers through a program he'd fed into his computer. He came up with two initial conclusions. "I'm damn sure he's a Native," he told Corporal Graham, "and I reckon he was 35 years old." To be safe, however, he officially recorded the remains as being a man in the 26- to 40-year age range, most likely Native, but possibly Caucasian. From his measurements of the hand bones and fingers he could also tell the man was right-handed.

When he'd finished his basic profile, he passed it and the skull over to Betty Gatliff so she could begin modelling with clay. Her experience had taught her the basic features of all faces. Mouths are usually equal to the width of the six top front teeth. Noses, on average, project out about three times the length of the nasal spine. Ears are usually the same length as noses. Skin and facial flesh are uniformly thick in males of a known age. Applying these basic formulas plus many more to the Tofield skull, Betty first covered it in flat-ended pins. These she used as guides as she applied her modelling clay until the skull was slowly transformed into the resemblance of a human face. She inserted glass eyes and completed the buildup of clay until a face of exactly the right proportions dictated by the skull stared back at her. It still looked like featureless, dull clay until she worked her cosmetic skills, adding eyelashes, eyebrows and hair. Her only disappointment was that skulls give no clues as to finer details, such as beards, freckles or warts. Finally, she was able to show Corporal Graham something no other investigator had yet seen in this baffling murder case—the face of the victim.

The Mountie had numerous photographs taken of the face and returned to Edmonton to launch a new wave of publicity. While the victim still had no name, he had acquired a nickname in the homicide unit. When the pictures of the face were released, the nickname "Septic Tank Sam" circulated with it.

Soon the face was staring out of newspapers across Canada, with the heaviest concentration of publicity being in Alberta. It produced a wave of potential new leads from people who thought they recognized an old friend or a missing relative. Investigators were kept busy checking every new tip. Months of careful work eliminated them all with no success.

By 1983, when the murder was still unsolved after six years, RCMP homicide investigators launched a renewed publicity drive calling for information, releasing details that they had previously kept secret. They revealed that the killers had rolled their victim up in a yellow bedsheet and tied the sheet with a nylon rope round his head and body. Detectives theorized that he'd been lying on the yellow sheet and had also been tied down to a bed at the unknown crime scene when they were torturing him.

The killers had used a small butane torch as the instrument of torture, the kind found in many home workshops across the province. Detectives deduced the victim must have been tied down because the burn marks on the sleeves of his shirt stopped just short of his wrists. More burn marks scorched the legs of his jeans, and one sock showed where they'd burned the sole of his foot during the cruel and deliberate torture. It looked like the killers had cut out the entire crotch area of his jeans with heavy-duty farm shears before sexually mutilating him. Finally, investigators revealed he'd been in the septic tank longer than at first thought, maybe even for a whole year. He may have been murdered as early as April 1976.

Still, the new information and publicity brought no results. The cutting-edge technology of facial reconstruction had been applied to Septic Tank Sam, yet almost a decade had passed since his murder and he still hadn't been identified.

Every successive team of detectives who moved into Edmonton RCMP's homicide unit inherited the case of Septic Tank Sam, but yet another decade passed without an identification being made. The passage of time was both a curse and a blessing. On one hand, every passing year meant potential witnesses might have moved away from the area; every passing decade meant some potential witnesses might have died. On the other hand, each new decade brought new scientific breakthroughs and technical advances that could be applied to the case.

In 1995, nearly 20 years after Septic Tank Sam surfaced, advances in computer technology offered investigators a new tool to help establish his identity. Forensic pathologists at the medical examiner's office in Edmonton had developed a new computer-sketching program that enabled them to construct a human face starting with only a skull. They had worked with University of Alberta anthropologist Dr. Owen Beatty, and in January 1995 they produced their computerized likeness of how the murder victim must have appeared. Sam now had his second face.

Edmonton RCMP constable Brad Siddell of the city's major crimes unit generated the next wave of publicity using the new "face of Sam" as the centrepiece. This time the computer was able to produce three images of Sam—one clean-shaven, one with a tidy moustache and one with a full beard. Siddell brimmed with confidence. "It's been used successfully in other cases. We're hoping it'll help us solve this one too," he said.

It brought an immediate wave of responses. At least 12 new leads came in from as far away as California and New Brunswick. Siddell and his team set about checking them all. One woman from California heard about Sam from a relative who'd seen the new publicity in Manitoba. She told police her brother had gone missing from Vancouver during that time period. The lead proved negative. A person in New Brunswick called to report a brother who had disappeared while travelling out west. That wasn't Sam either. Other leads came from across the prairies, from British Columbia to Saskatchewan. They were all negative too, as dental records ruled out every one of them. As in previous years, renewed publicity also brought out new potential suspects to be checked. Someone would call to say a friend said that so-and-so had been bragging that he'd killed someone and dumped him in a septic tank years earlier. Investigators tracked down and eliminated every suspect.

The new millennium brought Septic Tank Sam's third face. When Corporal Ed Lammerts first retrieved the gruesome remains out of the Tofield septic tank he knew it would be a difficult case. But even he could hardly have imagined he would make sergeant, have a long career, go into retirement—and years later still be watching with interest as successive generations of detectives tried to put a name to the victim. In 2000, Cyril Chan, a forensic artist with the Edmonton medical examiner's office, repeated the work done by Dr. Snow 21 years earlier. Once again Sam's remains were exhumed from their unmarked grave and Chan spent three weeks studying the skull. Then he rebuilt a clay face around it, with a few differences. This time Sam's mouth was open enough for people to see his teeth, and he had wooden eyeballs instead of glass. The new photographs were publicized. Chan was as confident as all the scientists before him had been. His office walls were festooned with newspaper clippings of successfully resolved cases, and he was aiming to add Septic Tank Sam to the list. When a family contacted investigators with details of a missing relative, it looked as if he might have made the breakthrough.

By 2001 detectives had another technological weapon in their armoury. The investigators before them did not even have fingerprints or blood samples of their victim to work with and had no sure-fire way of knowing if a particular missing person was their victim. Now there was DNA. Constable Jane Spaans was the new investigator. She had inherited the eight bulging boxes full of files on Sam in the Edmonton RCMP major crimes unit. The file now contained Sam's DNA profile. If a potential candidate surfaced, a quick comparison could confirm an exact match.

The family called in after seeing Chan's reconstruction of Sam's face. It looked like their missing relative, and all the details they provided fit the known facts. "This is the closest profile we've had to date," Constable Spaans told the media. "I don't want to say I'm 100 percent sure, but it's the most reasonable one." The story appeared under the headline: POLICE CLOSING IN ON SEPTIC TANK SAM'S ID.

Arrangements were made for DNA samples to be taken from the man's immediate family and even uncles, aunts and cousins. The process took several weeks, but when the comparisons were finally made, DNA ruled the man out.

To this day Septic Tank Sam hasn't been identified, but this most appalling of murders is seldom out of the newspapers. The *Tofield Mercury* brought out a special centennial edition in 2005 to celebrate the town's 100th birthday. The case of Septic Tank Sam, the town's most baffling and celebrated murder investigation, commanded an entire page. Nowadays, the murder file is housed in two complete filing cabinets in the Tofield RCMP detachment. Sergeant Jim Warren from Tofield talked about the case late in 2005 in another front-page feature carried by the *Tofield Mercury*. He hadn't given up hope that this murder might still be preying on someone's conscience, and they might come forward to unburden themselves of their guilt.

But when I talked with Dr. Owen Beatty, who'd worked on the case years earlier, he raised the interesting point that the murder might already be beyond solving because of the time that had elapsed. If the victim had been 35 years old when he was murdered in 1976 (as Dr. Snow had estimated), it might be reasonably supposed that the men who murdered him were about his age or older. They would now be at least 65 years of age, or even older. If witnesses were around Sam's age, they too would be nearly 70 years old. Anthropologists had calculated the age range of the victim as anywhere from 21 to 45 years. If he'd been 45 years old when murdered, and those around him were the same age, they would now be at least 75 years old. It's quite possible the killers may have already died. The chances of the victim's parents still being alive are even more remote. They would have to be in their 90s or approaching 100 years old.

There has to come a time when, as Dr. Beatty describes it, a case ceases to be "forensically active." The case is then labelled "historically interesting." The line is drawn when there is no chance that anyone connected with the case is still alive. That line hasn't been reached yet, but it's fast approaching. Generations of homicide investigators have thrown every available technological resource at trying to identify the victim. The Mounties at Tofield promise the case is still open today. In fact, if you have the vital information they seek, they are waiting for your call.

Note: For those readers who wonder, Corporal Jamie Graham of Edmonton RCMP in this story is the same officer appointed chief of police in Victoria in 2008, after previously serving as the chief of police in Vancouver from 2002 to 2007.

5

The Hand of God

THE BLACKENED GROUND CRUNCHED UNDERFOOT as a lone man walked where a forest fire had scorched the land. Suddenly, he stopped. There at his feet lay a tiny red rubber boot, half-charred by the flames. He stooped and picked it up, then raised his eyes to the heavens as if communicating with God.

In the hours that followed, teams of professionals found a few scattered bones of a child nearby. But it wasn't just any man who'd discovered the little red boot. This was a father who'd found the earthly remains of his own son. And for him to have made his find on this precise day was incredible. His was one of the most amazing stories ever to lead to such a revelation and discovery.

The scorched ground was in a remote area deep in the foothills of the Rockies on the Sunchild First Nation Reserve northwest of Rocky Mountain House, and more than 220 kilometres west of Edmonton. Rodger Rinker and his wife, Karen, were missionaries on the reserve, where they lived with their five children. The Rinkers had enjoyed a long association with the Sunchild Reserve, first moving there in 1975. They moved away five years later, travelling north to Old Crow in the Yukon Territory inside the Arctic Circle. They returned in 1986, after hearing that the Sunchild Reserve had been without a missionary for several years. At first they lived in a tent, until the worst flood in the area's history forced them to relocate to higher ground, which was where they built their church and their home. The family moved into their new house over Christmas 1986.

On May 6, 1987, Rodger was away on a trip to the United States, and little Jesse, his son, was playing by himself near the house. The two-and-a-half-year-old, flaxen-haired child often played there contentedly for hours. But when his mother went looking for him on this Monday afternoon, she couldn't find him anywhere. It didn't worry her for the first few minutes. The reserve wasn't like a big city with cars and people rushing by—people who might snatch a kid off the street. This was a very remote spot hewn out of dense forest. Days could pass without the Rinkers seeing anyone. If they did have a visitor, it was usually someone they knew from the reserve. At that moment, there probably wasn't another person other than Karen, her children and a few reserve residents within miles of their home.

Karen searched in the house, under the house, around the yard and in all Jesse's favourite play areas. Earlier that afternoon, one of Jesse's older brothers had walked away from the house along a lane through the heavy forest near the Baptiste River, which runs through the reserve. Someone thought they'd seen Jesse walking the same lane by himself. Perhaps he'd decided to follow his brother. They searched the lane, but he was nowhere to be found. Now Karen did start to worry. She called for help, and by 4:30 p.m. around 25 people from the reserve were beating the bush and calling Jesse's name. It wasn't easy. This was dense forest with thick scrubland and tall bushes. By nightfall they had found no trace of the toddler.

When he was informed that Jesse was missing, Rodger cut short his trip to Iowa and flew back immediately. By the next day he was home and the search party had increased to 100 people. Members of the Sunchild and O'Chiese Bands turned out, together with Alberta forestry workers, provincial park rangers, Alberta Fish and Wildlife personnel and nine members of the RCMP. Rocky Mountain House RCMP constable Richard Smith was searchmaster and led the entire group. Many of these people were professionally trained searchers, and it was an intensive hunt.

One searcher, Fred Dumais, who had been among the first to start looking on Monday, collapsed on Tuesday after searching non-stop for 24 hours. Fred had nine children at home and took the loss of anyone's child as a devastating blow. He was carried home to his place on the reserve, where a prayer meeting was held for little Jesse at Fred's bedside.

On the first full day of the search, teams covered two and a half square kilometres. The next day they intended to widen the search and tackle the Baptiste River and Coyote Creek, in case Jesse had fallen in the water. When the search for Jesse hit the media, it prompted an amazing public response. Volunteers flocked to the reserve to help, until more than 140 people were out looking for him. Soldiers in the British Army who were based at Nordegg, south of Rocky Mountain House, had been on military exercises nearby and were ordered into the search area to assist. The police brought in tracker dogs, and officers used infrared camera equipment from a police helicopter. Other officers dragged the Baptiste River from inflatable dinghies while scuba divers searched in the water, but no sign of the toddler was found.

On the third day of the search, a black pickup truck screeched to a halt at the command centre. A burly, heavily bearded man jumped out and sought out the search leader. He quickly explained that he was a licensed bear hunter and had just shot dead a black bear right in the heart of the area where Jesse had disappeared. He feared the bear may have eaten the little boy, and he'd brought it to the command centre to be opened up and examined. Such a suggestion had to be taken seriously, but needed to be handled with some delicacy. Rodger was near the command post at the time, but luckily hadn't heard yet what was happening. The RCMP searchmaster directed the truck to an area behind the command centre, out of the view of searchers and, more importantly, away from Jesse's father. Carefully, the bear was opened up. To the relief of everyone there, no human remains were found inside the animal.

The British soldiers brought a special expertise that the search organizers thought could help find Jesse. Very near the spot where he was last seen, several medium-sized lakes spread across the landscape. These had been formed over the years by beavers damming the nearby Baptiste River. It would be a huge operation to search every part of each lake, but there was one quicker way to solve the problem. If the army could blow up the beaver dams, the water would drain away. Strict safety precautions were taken and searchers were kept away from the dams. Sticks of dynamite were placed and the army blew the dams to pieces. The water drained off as predicted, but Jesse wasn't there.

Then one of the British soldiers finally found tangible evidence, something everyone had been seeking. What he had stumbled on had serious implications—it looked very much like a freshly dug shallow grave, exactly the right size for the body of a toddler. Jesse must have met with violence. His killer must have buried him, and now the army's diligent searching was about to reveal the crime.

With heavy hearts, a small group of RCMP officers and

senior British army officers followed the soldier into a clearing in the forest where they were about to investigate the gravesite. Suddenly, the group was confronted by one of the O'Chiese elders, who intercepted them. They couldn't go there, he told them. What the soldier had discovered was indeed the fresh grave of a child, but it wasn't Jesse. This was the sacred burial ground of the O'Chiese tribe, and this was the grave of one of their children who had died recently.

Every day for a week the volunteers came with unflagging hope and determination. They came from the nearby communities of Rocky Mountain House and Leslieville, and from halfway across Alberta—Calgary, Edmonton, Ponoka, Stettler, Red Deer and Olds. A large group from the Mennonite church in Stettler swelled the search parties. Most searchers were parents who said if their child were missing, they would appreciate others helping them to search. The whole team experienced a massive outpouring of emotion as they joined together to look for the toddler. It was all coordinated by the professionals, who made sure that the critical zone, within two kilometres of where Jesse was last seen, was scoured four times in that first week.

After several days, and for the first time, Jesse's parents voiced a different theory on the toddler's disappearance. Perhaps he wasn't out there in the bush. Perhaps, after all, there had been some stranger on the reserve the day Jesse went missing. "A kid just doesn't disappear. If he's not out in the bush then I think he may very well be alive with someone else," said Karen.

Jesse possibly abducted? It might explain why no trace of him had been found despite the intense hunt by hundreds of people. But it also might just be the last desperate expression of hope for the couple. Jesse's parents were surviving their ordeal purely on the power of prayer, with their unwavering faith pulling them through.

Nearly two weeks into the search, Rodger Rinker came to the conclusion that a stranger had definitely snatched Jesse. He made an emotional appeal for the kidnapper to return the boy and relieve family members of their agony. In his eyes, the search area was now one huge crime scene. Rodger revealed new information. On the day Jesse disappeared, several people remembered they had seen a strange vehicle on the reserve. Rodger's experience told him that only three kinds of people ever ventured onto the reserve—band members who lived there, people working in the forestlands, or strangers. And strangers were so rare, he said, that his family never saw more than one vehicle a week. Yet, coincidentally, a strange vehicle was seen in the area on the very day Jesse disappeared. Rodger's theory was gaining strength with the police as well. Corporal Glen Trites said the Mounties were becoming more and more convinced it was possible that Jesse had been snatched, since the ground searches for him had produced absolutely no clues.

Finally, after more than two weeks, the search was called

off on May 19. But the police investigation carried on. Officers from Rocky Mountain House were joined by others from Red Deer as they interviewed numerous people. Still, Rodger Rinker was unhappy because he felt the police had let things slip. Halfway through June he complained to the media that RCMP weren't working hard enough to find the stranger who may have snatched Jesse. Sergeant Ron Wesner defended his team's effort. He revealed that they had discovered quite a bit about the strange vehicle on the reserve that day. It was a small, red, foreign-made model with a white camper. The driver, who'd been seen collecting bottles, was around 45 to 50 years old.

Now, nothing could shake the Rinkers' belief that someone had taken Jesse, and they appealed to the kidnappers to have a change of heart and return the boy to them. The family extended their search outside the province. Rodger travelled to Saskatchewan to the east, British Columbia to the west and several American states to the south, distributing posters showing Jesse's smiling face and tousled hair. He hoped that someone would recognize his boy. The Calgary-based Missing Children Society of Canada distributed 5,000 posters of Jesse throughout Alberta.

Five months later, on November 14, 1987, an incredible phone call turned their lives upside down. Police in Edmonton had an abandoned toddler at the station. He looked a lot like Jesse, and all the circumstances led to the optimistic assumption that it was Jesse who had been handed over to authorities. After all, no one else had reported a little boy missing.

Even before the Rinkers left Rocky Mountain House to race to Edmonton, they were given details about the toddler over the phone that confirmed, in their minds, that Jesse had been found. Every detail matched what they knew about Jesse. They could tell the police that Jesse had a burn scar on his back from when he bumped against the stove in their home. Police checked and confirmed the mark was there. The foundling needed to wear diapers, despite being nearly three years old, the same age as Jesse. The Rinkers said that Jesse had suffered a viral infection as a baby that had delayed his toilet training. In addition, the illness had held back his physical development as well as his emotional progress—another exact fit.

Edmonton city police officers said the little boy in their custody could only articulate the word "ice-cream." This was the strongest clincher of all for the Rinkers. Jesse had his own little language and certainly couldn't explain to anyone who he was or where he came from. But they knew he could say "ice-cream."

Police explained the odd circumstances around the discovery of the little boy. Two Native women had knocked on the door of a house in Edmonton and asked the woman inside, a complete stranger, if she could look after this little non-Native boy for 20 minutes. The woman took him inside while she waited for the two women, but they never returned. A few days later, the woman took the boy to the police, where one officer noticed the resemblance to Jesse. All along, it had been thought that if Jesse had been snatched off the reserve and was being held, perhaps by Native people, one of them might have a change of heart and turn him in anonymously. That's exactly what happened—well, almost.

A shattering disappointment awaited the Rinkers in Edmonton. The boy wasn't Jesse. By an amazing coincidence, he was the same age as Jesse, looked a lot like him and had a birthmark on his back where Jesse had a burn scar. Like Jesse, he couldn't communicate with words and was not toilet trained. Days later, police investigations revealed the other toddler was a two-and-a-half-year-old boy called Gary Moses.

Such an appalling disappointment might have destroyed other families in the Rinkers' situation, but their unshakeable faith in God sustained them. And a month later Karen and Rodger were blessed with twin girls, who helped a little to fill the void left by Jesse's disappearance. Rodger spoke to God daily and eventually came to understand that God had set a date by when his family would know for certain what happened to Jesse. God told Rodger he had set the date at a year and one month after the toddler disappeared. If the Lord was as good as his word, the Rinkers would have their answer on Sunday, June 4, 1988.

Something major happened on the Sunchild Reserve as

that date approached. Two weeks before the Rinkers' crucial Sunday, an enormous forest fire erupted not far from their home. Soon the wind-driven inferno was exploding through the tops of the fir trees and roaring through the dense, dry brush. The blaze blackened 8,000 hectares of land before a small army of firefighters brought it under control. Luckily, the wind had blown the flames away from the Rinkers' home, which had been spared. Fire officials believed it was deliberately set, but they never found a culprit.

Sunday, June 4, 1988, came and still the family had no word of Jesse. Karen ended the day in tears, devastated that their hopes had been dashed again. Rodger knew there was only one thing left for him to do. He went out from their home to walk along the scorched earth blackened by the fire and to talk to God. "I remonstrated with God," he said. "I complained bitterly to him about letting us down."

What happened in the next few seconds was utterly miraculous. As Rodger walked, still berating God, he saw a moose antler showing starkly white against the blackened earth. The antler seemed to be pointing in a direction, so Rodger followed. A little further along the black trail he saw a second antler, this one pointing in a new direction. Following the direction of the second antler, he saw a third. When he picked up the third moose antler and walked a few paces farther, he saw in the blackened soil a tiny red rubber boot, half-charred by the flames. Inside the boot was a faded white sock. Thus, exactly one year and one month after Jesse had disappeared, Rodger discovered his son's remains. "I was led there by the hand of God," he said.

Rodger raced home with the boot, and an hour later the RCMP had assembled a 25-man search team. Near where Rodger had found the boot, searchers found other pieces of clothing. A tracker dog soon discovered human bone fragments. After several days of forensic tests, the province's chief medical examiner in Edmonton, Dr. John Butt, confirmed what Rodger knew in his heart. The bone fragments and clothing were all that remained of Jesse.

As tragic and heartbreaking as it was, it was a relief for the Rinkers to know what had happened. Fearing their son had been alive in the hands of a kidnapper for 13 months was something they couldn't handle. Knowing Jesse was dead gave them "an incredible sense of loss and great suffering," but it was still a relief to have that knowledge.

The Rinker family held a funeral service on their beloved Sunchild Reserve, conducted by an Aboriginal minister from the Stoney Band. Then they buried Jesse in a small cemetery overlooking Moberly Lake on a remote Native settlement, 110 kilometres west of Dawson Creek, British Columbia, and about 600 kilometres northwest of Edmonton. Jesse had spent the first year of his life in the Moberly Lake settlement, and he was buried there alongside his brother James, who had been stillborn in January 1987.

Since then the Rinkers, from their base at Three Hills in central Alberta, have continued their calling. Their missionary work has provided the spiritual foundation for residents on two reserves, one at Rocky Mountain House in Alberta and the other at Old Crow in the Arctic.

All these years later one question remains. How could Jesse have been missed in the very heart of an area that had been searched by professional search teams at least four times? Rodger had found Jesse's boot about 15 metres from the bank of Coyote Creek, and his few remains had been located a further 80 metres away.

Rodger surmises that Jesse had probably fallen into the creek, and his body had become submerged up under the bank. Thick foliage and undergrowth would have hidden his body from anyone walking along the creek bank, as well as from those searching the creek itself. After the searches were called off, it's entirely possible that Jesse's body surfaced naturally and animals dispersed his bones far and wide in the undergrowth. The vital factor was the forest fire that was so fortuitous for the Rinkers. The blazing inferno ravaged the area, cleared the foliage and exposed the blackened ground—finally enabling Jesse's remains to be found on the very day that God foretold his fate would be revealed.

6

The Sewage Plant Skeleton

ALONE AND LONELY, THE HOMELESS man crawled into his desolate shelter in a deserted ravine not far from Calgary's sewage plant, away from the thousands of citizens in their snug, warm homes. What happened to him that night no one knows, but by morning he was dead. No one missed him. No one found his body.

Nothing much happened to that isolated stretch of land for nearly 20 years, until new work was started on the sewage plant in the 1980s. A team of men with bulldozers was ordered to fill in the ravine as part of the landscaping connected to its expansion. By this time, Calgary was burgeoning, and the Bonnybrook Sewage Treatment Plant needed upgrading.

By the 1990s, the city was really booming and the

sewage plant needed a second major expansion. Once again, backhoes were sent in to excavate new foundations for the bigger and better plant. But this time the work had barely begun when it came to a complete halt. One of the workmen saw a shoe deep down in the earth, and he thought he could see human bones inside it. It was November 2, 1992. Uniformed police officers were called, and they brought in the homicide detectives.

Workmen had already excavated a pit at least five metres deep in preparation for installing an electrical manhole when they made their grisly discovery. It brought a sudden stop to the $140 million operation, and from that minute on, the sewage plant construction site was transformed into a full-scale crime scene.

Initially, workers had taken no notice of the shoe deep down in the excavation. Their work had produced two large mounds of earth below ground level, and the shoe was only partially exposed. Supervisor John Vogel said boots, shoes and other items were often found, which explained why the shoe was ignored at first, probably for a couple of days. "Today, one of the men checked the shoe, found bones inside it, so we called the police," said Vogel.

Forensic specialists from the medical examiner's office and homicide unit detectives climbed down ladders into the excavation site to carefully sift through the remainder of the mound of earth. After two days of digging they had located almost enough bones to complete an entire human skeleton. They photographed every stage of their work and took measurements of the ground around it. Once the bones had been removed, detectives scoured the base of the excavation pit with metal detectors, seeking any clue that might be linked to the mystery body.

In the next few days, Dr. Anne Katzenberg, an anthropologist from the University of Calgary, and a radiologist joined forensic experts at the medical examiner's office to examine the bones. Homicide unit detectives were also at their side, as no one knew at this stage whether or not this was a murder victim.

After three weeks, the forensic scientists under Alberta's chief medical examiner, Dr. John Butt, announced their findings. These amounted to a few sparse personal clues and a huge gap in information about who the man was. In fact, one of the few things they knew was that the remains were that of a man. They didn't know if he was Caucasian, Asiatic or Native, but they knew he wasn't black. He was probably tall, between 5 feet 9 inches and 6 feet 1 inch, and probably had black hair and a beard. They could certainly tell he'd had a rough life, as several of his bones had been broken long before he died. He'd had a broken jaw surgically repaired and suffered broken ribs, a broken finger and broken bones in his right foot. They thought he probably wore dentures, as his lower jaw had no teeth.

Everything else about him was a blank. The two biggest mysteries were how and when he died. His skeleton yielded no clues as to whether or not he'd met a violent death. Inspector Ray McBrien, in charge of Calgary's major crimes unit, explained the timing of the man's death with the vague phrase "modern day, but not recent." The forensic scientists had studied the surgical treatment carried out on the jaw, trying to assess in which decade such dental work was typically performed. They tried to determine the decade from the style of his shoes. Of course, not knowing when he died, even to within 10 years either way, made any search of missing persons files very difficult. The files they did consult all came up negative.

The crime scene investigators first had to find out what had been on the site in the previous two decades, as their body was "not recent" and hadn't been placed there in the past few weeks. They turned to the City of Calgary Survey Division, whose files in city hall contained aerial photographs going back decades. Photographs showed that in the years prior to the 1980s, the place where the body was found had been a heavily overgrown ravine. It was well documented in the city records that the ravine had been filled in as part of the sewage plant expansion in 1982.

From these clues, investigators formulated a theory. Perhaps this man had been living rough in the ravine, certainly before 1982 and perhaps in the 1970s or even the 1960s. He may have been a vagrant, and he had probably led a violent life. It was all so vague, not much more than an intelligent guess. Their only real hope was to appeal to the public for any information that might help them. It was probably the most optimistic appeal for help McBrien had ever put out. His team was looking for details on a man they couldn't describe, who may have been living in a ravine 10 or 20 years earlier as a homeless vagabond, and who therefore had no close family. Not surprisingly, by the end of 1992 the appeal had produced no results. But unknown to the crime scene investigators, the appeal had sparked a chain of events that was to bring a remarkable breakthrough, thanks to the undying love of a daughter.

For 24 years, Calgarian Corinne Boudreau had wondered what had happened to her father. It was a difficult situation for Corinne and her six siblings, who had all grown up and gone their separate ways. Their dad, an old soldier who'd served his country in the Second World War, had adopted a transient lifestyle, often disappearing for many months on end. Sometimes he'd be in Calgary, sometimes in Edmonton, often travelling between the two cities and seldom keeping in contact. They knew he was a tough, hard-drinking man who could look after himself. It would take someone special to beat him in a fight. They also knew some of his rougher scraps had left him with a few broken bones.

For Corinne, it was almost impossible to know at any given time whether her father was away for a few months in Edmonton, just wandering, or had disappeared altogether. But in February 1969, officials at the Colonel Belcher Hospital in Calgary contacted the family. They told Corinne that her dad, who was then 57 years old, hadn't picked up his armed forces pension cheque. Corinne knew the pension was her father's only income. No matter where his wanderings took him, he never missed his pension cheque. But from February onwards he never turned up at the hospital, and he never picked up another cheque.

Corinne, the eldest daughter, was worried. Her older brother, Dennis, shared her concerns as the months turned into years without any word from their father. Between them, the two siblings chased down any lead that might have given them a clue to his whereabouts. Throughout the 1970s, they kept their father in their thoughts, hoping he might still be alive. During the 1980s, they still kept him in mind, but knew that with the passing of 20 years any chance of discovering what had happened to him was long gone. Obviously, he was dead and whatever had befallen him could have happened almost anywhere in Alberta. They were resigned never to know the answer.

So when Corinne and Dennis read in the local newspaper on November 3, 1991, that human remains had been found near a sewage plant, they wondered if this might be their father. They decided to watch the papers in the next few days to see if more details might be released. By the end of November, what they read in the paper gave them much more hope. "When we heard the body may have been there for 20 years and had suffered various broken bones, we felt straight away it was probably Dad," said Dennis.

"I had a fear and a hope it was him," said Corinne, who started making her own inquiries without at first going to the police or the medical examiner's office. She began with the Department of National Defence, asking staff at the archives department if they had any medical records relating to her father. The archivists said they did have records, but they couldn't release them without a death certificate. Corrine was in a classic "catch 22" situation. She couldn't get a death certificate unless the records were able to prove her father was dead. And she couldn't get the records until she produced a death certificate.

She turned to Calgary MP Harvie Andre and explained her dilemma to him. Under pressure from the MP, the military authorities relented and agreed that the medical records of Corinne's father could be sent to the Calgary medical examiner's office for examination. Amazingly, dental X-rays meticulously kept by Veterans Affairs Canada showed that Corinne's father had had his jawbone wired together in a certain way when he was a young man. Forensic pathologists compared the X-rays to the jawbone from the sewage plant and found they were a perfect match. The remains were those of Corinne's father, Albert James Boudreau.

Two days after the match was made, on Friday, February 5, 1993, Corinne was at work in an office supporting the homeless when an RCMP officer and an investigator from the medical examiner's office walked in and broke the news she had waited 24 years to hear. "I lost my breath, then relief came over me and all I could say was, 'Thank you, Thank you, Thank you,'" Corinne recounted.

Corinne knew all about her dad's broken jaw. That had happened when he was a coal miner after the war. Someone busted his jaw during a union battle, and it had to be wired up. She thought it a remarkable twist of fate that if he hadn't got into that fight, his remains may still not have been identified.

Dr. Butt was full of praise for the meticulous care taken by the Veterans Affairs Canada office to preserve the medical records of war veterans. Their records showed Albert Boudreau, born in northern Alberta in 1911, enlisted in the army in Calgary at the outbreak of war in 1939 and was discharged when he was wounded in 1944. He had served in an artillery unit protecting Prince Rupert, British Columbia. This was at a period of the war when the port was a crucial north Pacific supply, storage and distribution centre for American and Canadian military forces. The vital dental X-ray was taken when his jaw was wired up in 1958, and their last record of him being alive was in 1968. Shortly after that he stopped picking up his army pension.

"This whole matter was only concluded by the remarkable availability of long-standing X-rays," said Dr. Butt. He pointed out that most X-rays are destroyed after a number of years, with the exception of those held by the Veterans Affairs Canada office.

Corinne and Dennis were relieved to have closure,

knowing at last what had happened to their father. Their family members would now have a gravestone to visit and a place to meditate, said Corinne. "It is a relief to know his spirit is with the Great Spirit," said Dennis.

But the story wasn't complete for the crime scene investigators, who still didn't know how Albert Boudreau had died. Detective Cal Johnston of the homicide unit said his death would probably always remain a mystery. Someone may have murdered him. He may have got drunk, fallen and injured himself and died. He may have passed out and died of exposure. However he died, the evidence showed the most likely chain of events was that he probably met his end in his makeshift transient's home in the grassy ravine near the sewage plant in the winter of 1968. His remains would have decomposed into the ground unseen. For 14 years nothing disturbed that ravine. Then in 1982, bulldozers filled it in during landscaping work. Still unseen, his remains lay buried under the ground for another 10 years, until the new excavation work revealed them.

Corinne had the last, sad word. "That's a horrible way for someone to die," she said, "alone, homeless and forgotten."

7

The Prophet
of Death

AND JACOB, THE SELF-PROCLAIMED prophet of God, led Eda, his devoted disciple, into the wilderness where they would fast to cleanse themselves in the presence of the Lord.

The next time Jacob went into the wilderness five months later, he led a posse of detectives and RCMP officers to the spot where he had buried the mortal remains of his beloved disciple. This cleft in a rock on a mountainous stretch of wilderness above Exshaw in southern Alberta quickly became the centrepiece of one of the most bizarre crime scenes most of these officers would ever encounter.

Usually, human remains found in shallow graves in remote locations are a complete mystery. It often takes months to establish who the victim was, and some remains are never identified. In contrast, this case seemed at first to be very straightforward. Right from the start, the police knew the remains were those of Eda Dianne Lee, a 26-year-old mother of a young child. What's more, they knew who'd buried her there. Jason Samuel "Jacob" Lee, Eda's 30-year-old husband, had brought her to this place—and confessed that he had fashioned her grave himself.

It was Sunday, March 5, 2000, and police had been searching for Eda for five months since she had been reported missing by her friends. It seemed as if police had found the answer right there on the mountain. But the biggest mystery of all still remained. How had Eda died? Was foul play involved? Was this truly a crime scene? What crime had been committed? They had no idea an amazing investigation was about to unfold before them.

Calgary police detective Scott Buchanan was the first officer to stumble into the nearly unbelievable world of weird religion and cult behaviour that was behind this mysterious death. He and his partner, Detective Len Minello, had come into the picture five months earlier, in November 1999, when a couple who had been living on the streets of Calgary were reported missing by friends—an ordinary enough start to what became an extraordinary case. These friends knew that Jacob and Eda were fervently engrossed in religious beliefs that dominated their entire lives, and they started to worry when the couple disappeared in October. All agreed the two were inseparable, so new alarm bells started ringing when later they thought they'd seen Jacob alone, without Eda at his side.

For five months, the two detectives worked on the missing persons case, until they finally found Jacob. When Buchanan began interviewing him, he could hardly believe his ears. The case-hardened detective spent 27 hours talking with Jacob and later said he'd never heard a story like it in his entire 20-year career.

To start with, Jacob wasn't the man's real name. He had chosen to take the name of the son of Isaac in the Bible, the book that governed his whole life. He and Eda lived rough on Calgary's streets, having no use for society, money or work. Jacob believed if God intended them to eat, he would provide food. In the Bible, Jacob was "always in touch with God and surrounded by visions, dreams, and even angels." In the back streets of Calgary, Jacob was always in touch with God as well. He told Buchanan he spoke privately with God every day, receiving guidance on where and how he and Eda would get food, if any, that day.

Not only did Jacob Lee spend many hours every day studying the Bible, he was rewriting it to better reflect his religious beliefs. His version of the Bible was so extreme and radical that even church leaders couldn't accept it. Jacob and Eda, one-time members of the Church of Jesus Christ of Latter-day Saints, had been excommunicated for their views. Jacob was angry with the Mormon Church, which he said had watered down the true meaning of the scriptures.

Buchanan learned that church leaders weren't the only ones disturbed by the teachings of Jacob. Some people close to the self-proclaimed prophet were scared he would one day exercise his power and become a notorious cult leader exhorting disciples to follow him to disaster for his beliefs. But Eda wasn't scared. She followed him enthusiastically and revered him.

Even on the day Jacob came to her saying that God had spoken to him and had commanded the couple to fast in the wilderness for 40 days and nights—as Jesus had done— Eda didn't question him. She believed Jacob's every word. Right away, she and her prophet set off hitchhiking along the Trans-Canada Highway to Canmore, as God had directed. From there the couple hiked to a high, mountainous plateau above Exshaw, where the fast began. God had given Jacob precise instructions for the fast. One commandment forbade them to drink water, and they obeyed it steadfastly. For six days and nights nothing passed their lips.

There came a time when Jacob feared he was so weak he might die. Eda told him if that happened she would bury his body right there, high on God's mountain. Soon it became obvious that it wasn't Jacob who was fading, but Eda, who was nearly at death's door. That morning God spoke to Jacob again and gave him permission to go fetch water for Eda. She was too weak to move, so Jacob clambered down the mountain to a stream to fetch water, which took nearly half the day. When he returned to their fasting place high on the mountain, Jacob found he was too late. He told Buchanan that when he got there he found Eda had died.

Now police had Jacob's explanation of how Eda had passed away. No murder, no violence, and certainly not directly by his hand. Forensic pathologists in the medical examiner's office would have to determine if his story was true or false, if Eda's body was ever found. But what Jacob had done after Eda died definitely needed investigating by police, whatever he said.

Jacob had kept Eda's death a secret for five months, but in his own eyes he'd done nothing wrong. When he found Eda dead he believed immediately she had gone to be with God in a better place. He even assured himself this was God's will, prompting him to perform a burial ceremony for his disciple right there on the mountain. He said he had carefully dressed her body in what he described as religious clothing, wrapped it in a sleeping bag and placed it in a natural crevice on the mountainside.

Buchanan's suspicions were aroused. Here was a man who admitted going into a remote mountainous area with a woman, and who returned alone some time later. For five months he never mentioned the woman again. When detectives questioned him, he said he did nothing wrong, but her remains were somewhere out there in the wilderness.

What happened next shocked Buchanan and his partner. Out of the blue, Jacob volunteered to take them to the body. So it was that Buchanan and other Calgary city police and

RCMP officers followed Jacob back up the mountain behind Exshaw, where they found Eda's remains exactly as Jacob had described. Of course, police couldn't take Jacob's word for everything, so forensic scientists, crime scene investigators and the medical examiner's office were brought into the case.

Within three days, forensic pathologists at the medical examiner's office had decided that Jacob was apparently speaking the truth. Staff Sergeant Pat Kamenka put out a series of press releases from the Canmore RCMP detachment outlining the medical examiner's results. A forensic odontologist had compared dental records and confirmed the remains were Eda's. The medical examiner said that, however she had met her death, it wasn't a homicide; she had died of dehydration. Despite these findings, police decided a crime had been committed.

"The couple had gone into the woods to fast and during this time Eda passed away," said the staff sergeant. "Mr. Lee [Jacob] then buried the body and returned to Calgary without notifying the police of the death of his wife." Jacob was charged with unlawfully disposing of human remains and was remanded in custody to undergo psychiatric assessment to establish if he was fit to stand trial.

While Jacob was temporarily behind bars, a disturbing story surfaced about two more of his disciples. They had been snatched from his grasp by their relatives and friends shortly before it was feared he was about to take them into the mountains to fast. If Jacob's plans had come to pass, the disciples would have taken their two young children, one of them a newborn baby, with them into the wilderness. This incident happened in the months after Eda had died on the mountain, when no one knew she was there, when Jacob was keeping her death a secret, and when he was clearly recruiting new disciples to follow him.

One day, a couple driving to Edmonton picked up a hitchhiker. His religious fervour and charismatic character overwhelmed the couple as they talked in the car. By the time they reached Edmonton he had converted them to his ways and persuaded them to let him live with them. "It was scary," said the couple's closest friend in Calgary, who would later be instrumental in helping to snatch the two new disciples away from their leader.

Jacob gave his new female disciple the name of Rachel, forbidding her to use her old name. In the Bible, Rachel was Jacob's second wife. The self-proclaimed prophet's strict rules about fasting were imposed on Rachel, which was alarming as she was about to give birth to the couple's second child. Her Calgary friend was horrified to discover that there was no food in her house and no money for food, as the new disciples had handed over all their cash to Jacob. But things were about to get much worse.

The two new disciples started selling all their possessions, turning everything they owned into cash and handing it over to Jacob. They had been running a successful business in Calgary, but to their friend's amazement, they suddenly sold it, and all the proceeds went to their new master. They even sold their Christmas presents to provide cash to buy the knapsacks that they would need during their upcoming fast in the mountains.

What happened next was so drastic it prompted the friend to take action. Jacob had talked with God one day and told Rachel she must have her baby at home as God didn't believe in hospitals. The friend couldn't stand by any longer. She was in a race against time to save the couple and their unborn baby. She knew her friends' parents all lived in Manitoba. She called them, warning them of what was taking place and asking them to help her.

The family members drove straight from Manitoba to Calgary and arrived just as Rachel started going into labour. They ignored Jacob's orders and raced her to the hospital, where her baby was delivered safely. Several weeks later, Rachel, her 18-month-old son and her newborn baby all disappeared and were reported to police as missing persons. Just as mysteriously, they returned after seven days.

Jacob's impact on the couple's lives had been totally disruptive. Rachel returned to Manitoba where her two children were placed in the custody of their grandparents. Her husband was admitted to the psychiatric ward of a Calgary hospital, where one day a "brother" he never had tricked his way into the ward to visit him. It was Jacob, still trying to maintain his hold over his disciple. Back in Manitoba, the couple's relatives were relieved they had managed to intervene. Thanks to the warning from the friend in Calgary, they arrived before Jacob could lead their loved ones and the two children on another fast into the mountains. It had been a close call.

A great deal more about the background to this odd case was revealed on the day of Eda's funeral, on March 18, 2000. From his jail cell that day, still awaiting his first appearance in court, Jacob talked to the media at length about his religious beliefs, his life with Eda and how she had died. That day, Eda's family transformed her funeral into a musical celebration of her life, for she had been a talented musician. She played the violin at age three and the piano at eight. She earned a scholarship to the University of Calgary and taught violin for seven years. At the service, her musically gifted family members played Eda's compositions and the choir sang a song she'd once asked to be sung at her funeral.

In his eulogy, Eda's father said that her musical virtuosity had brought "tranquillity to my soul" and "happiness to our family." Another tribute to her musical life came in a letter from Jacob's mother in Tennessee, where she was looking after the couple's son, Joseph. She recalled that Eda and Jacob wrote music and sang songs together, and that they had recorded a tape to be saved for their son to hear. Of Eda, she wrote, "Her sweet spirit lives on in her son, and her memory and her love for him lives on in our hearts."

Eda's great-uncle, LaMont Matkin, put her marriage to Jacob and her strange death into context, remembering that the couple had been excommunicated only three years earlier from the very church where the funeral service was now being conducted. He used carefully chosen words. "Eda was beguiled and deceived by someone who lost the understanding of the sacred role of God in a marriage," he told the mourners. Later that day, Eda was buried after a short graveside service in Cardston, in southern Alberta.

Jacob didn't agree with what Eda's great-uncle had said. At the very moment family members and mourners were celebrating Eda's life in the church, he sat in his Calgary Remand Centre cell explaining his views on life and how they set him apart from other men. To begin with, he said, Eda wouldn't have appreciated having a large funeral such as the one her family had organized. He claimed Eda had wanted a simple burial with no grave marker—exactly like the one he gave her on the mountainside above Exshaw. "I said a prayer and dedicated the site where she was placed and I felt it was done appropriately," said the self-proclaimed prophet of God.

Jacob went on to say that after they had been excommunicated by the Mormon Church, he and Eda had lived for years on the streets of Calgary, sleeping under bridges, in ditches or in the bush. Though the city's soup kitchens were available to them, they only once had a meal there, believing that God would provide sustenance. Sometimes God guided them to find food in trash cans in back alleys. Their normal day would be a non-stop round of praying, reading the scriptures and moving on to find a new sleeping place for the night.

But mostly, their purpose in life was to live by their interpretation of the Gospels and to preach the word to everyone they met. Jacob likened it to "God sending out apostles to preach to the people," taking no money or food with them. "Just go and accept whatever people provide for you, just receive that and be grateful. God will provide." The couple hitchhiked everywhere and preached to anyone who would listen.

Eda's family members weren't impressed by Jacob. Her parents knew that their university-educated and musically talented daughter sometimes suffered depression and needed a nutritious diet and regular sleep. They had been shocked when Jacob persuaded Eda to marry him after they'd only known each other three weeks. And they were worried when shortly before the couple left for their "spiritually cleansing experience" on the mountaintop, Eda called them to apologize for everything. They never saw her alive again.

From his remand centre cell Jacob repeated that he really was a prophet and that he was not upset at Eda's death. "If God had wanted her to live he would have sustained her long enough for me to give her water. I feel very much at peace with it," he said. Despite professing to be a prophet, Jacob didn't like being branded a "cult leader." He drew a distinction between deliberately going out to aggressively recruit people to follow him, which he denied, and letting people come to him, listen to him and learn his teachings, which he admitted. One of his strict rules was that no one could ever take his photograph, so that no image of him could exist. But on the day he chose to talk to the media, he produced a carefully posed photograph of himself in a flowing white robe with a religious symbol of faith round his neck, and his hands clasped in his lap as if in prayer. He had a short beard and moustache, and his long hair cascaded around his shoulders.

He looked very different a few days later when he appeared in Canmore provincial court charged with unlawfully disposing of Eda's remains. He was now clean-shaven, his luxurious locks cut short, and a black leather jacket replaced his flowing white robe. After a short hearing, Jason Samuel Lee (the court having dealt with him under his real name) was released on bail to appear the following month to face the charge.

A surprise awaited the media assembled outside the court. Jason, quickly reverting to being Jacob, stepped outside the building and made a peculiar speech of forgiveness from the courthouse steps. Jacob forgave the media—who had no idea they needed forgiving! "I publicly forgive all the people who've lied about this situation," he began. "I forgive all the media who have misrepresented the truth and publicized those lies and misrepresentations." He wouldn't elaborate on what he considered to be lies. He told the assembled media he had loved his wife very much. "I never forced her to do anything. What she did, she did out of her own choice, and I did out of my own choice." Then his lawyer drove him back to Calgary.

When the case was finally heard on May 31, 2000, Jason's lawyer, Joe Nahman, had struck a deal with the prosecution, which brought more pain to Eda's family. The serious charge of unlawfully disposing of his wife's remains was dropped, and instead Jason pleaded guilty to the lesser charge of failing to report her death.

A few new facts came out during the hearing. Nahman said the couple had spent their six-day fast in the wilderness singing hymns and reading the scriptures. Eda was as much attuned to their beliefs as Jason was, maybe even more so as she wanted to be totally reliant on Christ. On the day she had died, it had taken Jason six hours in a severely weakened state to fetch the water and get back to her side, where he was too late to save her. Judge John Reilly said he was satisfied Jason had committed no foul play in Eda's death and sentenced him to one day in jail. Such leniency outraged Eda's family. "Her parents are deeply hurt," said her great-uncle Matkin. "The one-day sentence is certainly inadequate, but what can we do?"

In the Bible, Jacob deceived his own family about his birthright. Eda's family members said they felt deceived by the justice system, and at her funeral Matkin told mourners she had been deceived by the man she had followed. There are those who felt it was entirely fitting that when he sought a new name for himself, Jason Lee chose to call himself Jacob—the great deceiver and manipulator.

CHAPTER

8

One Death—
Three Burials

It was like a nightmarish scene from a Hollywood horror movie, but this was no ghoulish film set. Amazingly, it was really happening just outside Calgary's city boundary. In the dead of night, lit only by flashlights, furtive figures dug a body out of a grave in a lonely cemetery. And right there, on the grass beside the black hole, a fully qualified forensic pathologist performed the most incredible autopsy ever done in all of Alberta, probably in all of Canada.

You can bet the authorities in Calgary didn't know what was taking place that night. Only two men knew—the man who ordered the unofficial exhumation and the pathologist who secretly flew in from the United States to carry out this man's macabre wishes.

The body raised from its resting place that night was that of an 84-year-old woman called Nora. She had died in the Calgary General Hospital on August 20, 1991. Hospital staff attributed her death to natural causes. This wasn't questioned by the medical authorities, who knew she had heart problems, or by her family members—except for one. Her son Bert, then 54 years old, was convinced some dreadful mistake by the hospital had cost his mother her life, and he insisted an autopsy be carried out. He said it would reveal exactly where the hospital had gone wrong. Autopsies aren't carried out on people who die of natural causes, so Calgary's medical examiner's office investigated every detail with Nora's physicians and the hospital staff. Convinced everything possible had been done for her, they were satisfied she had died of natural causes and refused to agree to Bert's demand for an autopsy.

Bert still disagreed. He turned to the courts and applied for a court-ordered autopsy to be undertaken, but the court turned him down as well. All this took time, and Nora's body still hadn't been buried. Most people who die naturally are buried in a few days at most. Finally, Calgary's medical officer of health stepped in and ordered that Nora be buried. On September 11, 1991, more than three weeks after she died, Nora was laid to rest in the Pine Creek Cemetery at De Winton, just outside the city's southern extremities.

But the medical examiner's office hadn't heard the last of Bert. He pressured staff so much that Alberta's chief medical examiner, Dr. John Butt, contacted Okotoks RCMP. The

Pine Creek Cemetery at De Winton was in their area, and Butt gave them an extraordinary warning. "Watch out," he told them. "There's a certain man who might go there one night and dig his mother up."

That's exactly what took place on the night of the Hollywood horror-movie scene. Nora hadn't been buried two weeks when Bert carried out his secret plan. He had found a fully qualified forensic pathologist in private practice in Oregon who agreed to perform a midnight autopsy at the graveside for cash.

For $1,800 plus his airfare and a few other expenses, Dr. William Brady agreed to come to Calgary and assist Bert in what he wanted most: to reveal how his mother had really died. The RCMP couldn't guard the cemetery every night, and on September 24, Bert and Dr. Brady carried out their ghoulish work unseen. Bert arrived complete with a makeshift coffin he knew he'd need later in the night. He even took photographs of the autopsy procedure so he would have evidence with which to confront the hospital.

It was all a great disappointment for him. The American pathologist could only confirm exactly what the hospital staff had said all along. Nora had died of natural causes. Before the sun came up, the two men placed Nora back in her grave for the second time. Bert, a painter and decorator who was skilled in carpentry, buried her this time in his home-made coffin. They then levelled the ground, hoping no one would know they had been there.

The Pine Creek Cemetery lay some distance from the main highway that leads south out of Calgary. This quiet little cemetery had been a serene and peaceful place ever since it was established in the early 1900s. So, what awaited the staff when they arrived at the cemetery the next day came as a terrible shock. As the morning sun rose in the sky, an unbelievable sight met their eyes. When Bert and his pathologist gravedigger had tried to level the ground in the dark they had driven all over other people's graves and caused serious upheaval and damage.

"It was a dreadful mess," said Ruth Hamilton, president of the cemetery management committee. Pretty soon the RCMP at Okotoks knew something macabre had taken place in the dead of night in the cemetery, and from Dr. Butt's warning they had a good idea what it was and who had done it.

There was only one way for them to confirm if their worst fears had been realized. They would have to exhume Nora's body and have her officially examined by the rightful authorities. This time Nora's exhumation was carried out with proper decorum and decency by RCMP officers. Then they transported her remains to the medical examiner's office in Calgary.

When he made his examination, it was obvious to Dr. Butt that what he had warned of had actually taken place. "I am appalled," he said. "A clandestine, sloppy autopsy was done by a man who has no licence to practice any form of medicine in this province. The whole thing from the start is bizarre. It is a disgrace."

Finally, after Dr. Butt had finished, and for the third time, Nora's body was lowered into her grave at the Pine Creek Cemetery, and this time it became her final resting place. But the controversy surrounding the awful indignities inflicted upon her body after she died had hardly started. The scandal reverberated in Canada and the United States after being stoked up yet again by Nora's son Bert.

No one knows why he did it. Bert chose several of the photographs he had taken that night and sent them to the *National Enquirer*, a tabloid newspaper in the United States. Worse still, he sent one to his older brother Wallace, who was devastated. "That's what I'm going to remember the rest of my life," said Wallace.

Authorities in Canada and the United States immediately began investigations to see if either Bert or Dr. Brady had broken any laws in either country. They wanted to know if action could be taken against them. Dr. Butt wanted something done, if only to prevent such a ghoulish thing from happening again. "This man came here on a fly-in fly-out job that kept him here one night. Does this mean anyone can go to a cemetery and dig up a body and slice it up?" he asked.

Canadian medical authorities led the battle. The fundamental rule in the Medical Professions Act of Alberta is that only doctors licensed in the province can perform medical acts, and that includes autopsies. Alberta's College of Physicians and Surgeons said Dr. Brady had no such licence and had clearly broken the code. They pointed out that any investigation that might lead to charges being laid must be carried out by the attorney general's office and the RCMP. They put the matter into the attorney general's hands right away. If Dr. Brady was found guilty of practising medicine without a licence, he could face a $1,000 fine or three months in prison.

With authorities gunning for him, Dr. Brady was quick to present his side of the story, explaining that he considered he'd done nothing wrong. He claimed he hadn't performed the autopsy just for the cash, as some had suggested, but for an honourable reason. A relative had approached him saying Canadian authorities had refused the family's wishes to have an autopsy. He had been "totally amazed" that a family in Canada could be denied an autopsy on a loved one if they sincerely wanted it. He had simply provided a service that he felt the family should never have been denied in the first place. He disagreed his work was "sloppy," saying he'd been thorough and careful and felt badly if Canadian patholo-gists were concerned about the standard of his autopsy.

Dr. Brady had a ready answer to the major criticism, which was that he didn't have a medical licence to perform the clandestine dissection. When he had crossed the border to enter Canada, he had told the border guards why he was going to Calgary. They granted him a work permit for a day.

In his eyes, the Canadians knew he was there to perform an autopsy and had granted him a permit to do it. "To the best of my knowledge it was a procedure approved by the authorities," he said.

His American medical superiors watched every development very closely. In the United States, Dr. Brady was accountable to the Oregon Board of Medical Examiners. Their chief investigator had made his own inquiries in Alberta to see if their man could be accused of "unethical or unprofessional conduct." After all, they said, if a Canadian pathologist came to Oregon in the middle of the night with no licence and no paperwork, dug up an American and did an autopsy alongside the grave, there would be total outrage.

They had good cause to be intensely interested. Dr. Brady had a history. Six years earlier, in 1985, he had been fired from his post as state medical examiner in Oregon after accusations that he was selling body parts. Medical authorities alleged Dr. Brady had been selling skin samples and pituitary glands to research agencies. They said he'd been salting the money away in a bank account designated for office holiday parties, and for buying furniture, copying machines and other supplies. Dr. Brady didn't think he'd done anything wrong that time either. He said the samples came from victims of aircraft crashes or car wrecks, or from bodies that were going to be cremated anyway. He claimed that all the money was used to provide improved facilities in his office. A report into his activities also alleged he'd been profiting by carrying out private autopsies during his normal office hours.

Dr. Brady had been suspended while a special prosecutor launched a full-scale criminal investigation into what he'd been doing. The attorney general's department eventually decided that what he did may have been ethically wrong, but it was nothing criminal. It was wrong, they said, for the money to have gone into better office amenities, but there was no evidence to show Dr. Brady had used the money for himself. There was nothing to support a criminal prosecution.

Oregon's Ethics Commission then looked at Dr. Brady's activities, but decided it wouldn't fine him because he had already paid back more than $17,000 in restitution to the state. Nevertheless, they did fire him. His bosses considered that he had "knowingly violated public trust and confidence" for his activities over the previous 16 years, and they wanted him gone. But Dr. Brady had the last word. He sued for $300,000 damages, claiming he'd been fired without proper legal hearings into his case, and he won. A federal jury ruled his constitutional rights had been denied when he was fired. Later, when Oregon officials took the case to the United States Supreme Court, it ruled in favour of Dr. Brady as well.

Back in Canada, the attorney general's department had given the case of Nora's clandestine autopsy to the Okotoks RCMP for investigation. When their report arrived, the way forward was clear. There would be no criminal charges against Dr. Brady in Alberta either. It didn't matter whether he had a medical licence or not. He had been granted a visa to enter Canada, and on the visa he clearly stated his purpose was to carry out an autopsy. Case closed.

One question remained. If the good doctor hadn't done anything wrong in law, what about Bert? Had he broken any laws? His brother Wallace and the rest of the family tried to have Bert charged with desecrating their mother's gravesite, which was a criminal offence, but the attorney general's office ruled against such a charge being laid. It was the lawyers' opinion that there was no criminal intent in Bert's mind when he organized the autopsy. There was no evidence that he had intended an "unlawful indignity" to his mother's remains.

On March 5, 1992, Bert was committed for psychiatric assessment to Calgary General Hospital under a mental health warrant. This was a result of his inexplicable actions in taking those distressing photographs of the autopsy and then sending them to his brother and the media. Wallace was left distraught by the whole amazing sequence of events. His beloved mother had been dug up from her grave twice, buried three times, money had changed hands, yet no charges were ever laid against the two men responsible for the bizarre incidents.

CHAPTER

9

"Get Help! They're Going to Kill Me!"

WHEN POLICE DIG UP MURDER victims from shallow graves, they usually follow up with a blaze of publicity to help establish the identity of the remains. This time there was total silence. It was top secret. No one in Alberta knew, save the RCMP officers wielding the shovels—and the man who'd led them there.

No one noticed the RCMP vehicles at the gravesite crime scene in a remote stretch of wilderness at Sibbald Flats, near Kananaskis Country in the foothills of Alberta's Rocky Mountains. It was March 10, 1993. The Mounties lifted the skeleton out of the ground, unseen by prying eyes. They took it away, identified the murder victim, but told no one. Not even the man's family.

What a contrast from the scene a year before. When Calgary city police dug up Sherwin Fettig from a shallow grave northwest of Cochrane, they invited the media along for the day, photographers included. They aimed to use the publicity to unnerve the killer and panic him into revealing his hand.

In this case, the RCMP investigators were in the rare position of knowing a great deal about the skeleton they had just recovered, even before they lifted him out of the ground. They knew his identity; they even knew who had murdered him, how and why. But still it suited their purposes to let no one know they had found him.

After more than a week of undercover work, they at last considered it safe to tell the man's family they'd found him. The victim was Gregory Kungel, who had been 23 years old when he disappeared three years earlier in September 1990. Now, the RCMP swore his family to secrecy. Gregory, from Medicine Hat, had moved to Calgary to find work in the construction industry. His father, James, was completely shocked at his son's death and mystified by the strange behaviour of the Mounties. All James Kungel knew was that Gregory had arranged to meet him in September 1990 in Medicine Hat, but hadn't turned up. Months passed and it was obvious to James that something bad had befallen his son. He reported him as a missing person in 1991 and heard no more about him until contacted by the RCMP.

Investigators told James not to publish any obituaries to

his son in the local newspapers and to have a very low-key funeral. Gregory was buried with none of his friends at the service—none of them knew he was dead. Two more weeks passed with the family enduring their enforced silence and the RCMP imposing its veil of secrecy. Only on April 2 did Calgary RCMP inspector Garry Fotheringham announce that police had found the skeleton of Gregory Kungel in a shallow grave, and that he'd been murdered. It was hardly "news" for the media, as Fotheringham revealed that police had made the discovery three weeks earlier. The *Calgary Herald* ran the story the next day under the headline: COPS KEPT MUM ON FINDING BODY.

So what was the big secret? The RCMP said the silence was to enable them to "take certain investigative steps." They certainly didn't have much trouble finding their suspect, Hermesh Erach Austin. They already had him in jail awaiting trial on charges of international drug smuggling. Now they charged him with the first-degree murder of Gregory Kungel.

RCMP detectives knew a great deal about Austin, going right back to the very day in 1990 when he murdered Kungel in cold blood. Several men witnessed the killing and the brutal torture that Kungel suffered beforehand. The story was as horrible as any the detectives had ever heard.

It started on a September night in 1990, with a cab driver carrying two passengers in downtown Calgary on a routine ride. Suddenly, an unknown stranger leaped into the cab, yelling, "Get me the hell out of here." Within seconds, a pickup truck rammed into the cab, and two burly strangers grabbed the distraught man back out into the road. As they took the struggling man away, he yelled, "Get help! They're going to kill me!" The cabbie quickly got out to write down the licence number of the truck. A third burly man immediately got out of the truck, threw the cabbie $300 and told him not to take down the number. The cabbie obeyed, and the three men drove off with their prisoner still yelling for help.

He didn't know it then, but the cabbie had witnessed the prelude to a dreadful murder. The fleeing stranger who was trying to escape the three men was Gregory Kungel, and his attackers were Hermesh Austin and two of his henchmen. Austin was a Calgary drug dealer, and the two bodybuilder giants were his enforcers. Austin's house had been burgled and $10,000 worth of cash and valuables stolen. Austin reckoned Kungel was the thief. The drug dealer, who was widely feared because of his reputation for extreme violence, was about to take his revenge.

The three men drove their prisoner to a deserted warehouse in a southeast Calgary industrial site where Austin tortured Kungel for hours. His feet were burned with an acetylene blowtorch, his hair was cut off and one of his hands was crushed in a vice. He was kicked and beaten with a hammer, a bat and a pipe, but he didn't die. For four days his tormentors kept him alive with painkillers.

On the fourth night, Austin decided it was time for his

victim to die. Kungel, with his head and feet bandaged, was bundled into a truck. Austin took four of his henchmen with him. Their two vehicles drove out to a deserted and remote spot at Sibbald Flats, 60 kilometres west of the city. Austin had already made sure that a shallow grave had been dug in readiness. In front of the four witnesses, Austin put two bullets in Kungel and stabbed him. After the corpse was dumped into the makeshift grave, Austin's men poured lime over the body and filled in the grave.

Austin, who was a powerfully built bodybuilder himself, had earned his reputation for violence even before the torture and slaying of Gregory Kungel. Two months earlier, he and two of his heavyweights had beaten up another man who'd crossed him. Kevin Sluth had accidentally cost Austin $30,000 worth of drugs. If the consequences hadn't been so serious it might almost have been funny.

Austin and his accomplices had entrusted a stash of cocaine to Sluth with instructions for him to guard it for them. On July 17, 1990, Sluth was in his apartment when there was a banging at the door. In a panic, fearing it was the police and that they would discover the drugs, Sluth quickly flushed $30,000 worth of Austin's best cocaine down the toilet. It turned out it was the TV cable repairman who was at the door.

Sluth confessed what he had done to Austin and his accomplices. Five days later, the angry drug dealer summoned Sluth and his girlfriend. While the girlfriend was forced to watch, Austin and two others beat Sluth so badly that he needed 39 stitches in hospital to close his wounds. To ensure Sluth never told hospital staff how he came by his injuries, Austin sent a "minder" to stay with him while he was being stitched up.

Eventually Sluth plucked up the courage to admit to police that he'd been beaten and who did it. Austin and one of his bodybuilders were charged and both pleaded guilty in court to aggravated assault in February 1992. The next day, in reporting that the drugs had gone down the toilet, the *Calgary Herald* couldn't resist a headline stating that the attackers were FLUSHED WITH ANGER, while the *Calgary Sun* had them FLUSHED WITH GUILT.

Austin naturally kept quiet about what else he had done in the period between beating up Sluth and going to court. The judge told him there was no place for "macho TV violence in real life" and jailed him for 18 months. No one in the courtroom, save Austin, knew his secret. Everyone thought the beating he had handed out to Sluth was the worst Austin had ever done. Only he and his henchmen knew there was another example of his handiwork lying undiscovered under the ground at Sibbald Flats.

Austin served his whole sentence with his secret intact. One might think that when he came out of prison he would have kept a low profile to avoid attracting attention. But that wasn't Austin's way. In 1992, RCMP drug investigators learned of a large-scale international drug-smuggling ring that was running cocaine from the Bahamas into Canada. The ring was bringing in big shipments of the drug on commercial flights into Toronto and Montreal and then running them to Calgary and Vancouver. Undercover drug detectives quickly learned that Austin was the brains behind the operation. He was kept under secret surveillance.

The two men who had dug the grave at Sibbald Flats back in 1990 were half-brothers. Now, in 1992, Austin used one of them, Darryl Milligan, as a courier to bring a shipment of cocaine into Canada from the Bahamas. Not long after making the run, Milligan disappeared, just as Kungel had before him. No one ever officially accused Austin of making Milligan disappear, but the man's half-brother, Fred Dickson, believed their drug-dealer boss was eliminating witnesses. He became very scared. In January 1993, he took a huge gamble, hoping to save his own neck. He went to the police and told them he had witnessed what had happened to Kungel.

This came as a shock to the RCMP. They had Austin under constant surveillance as he was still running his Bahamas drug-smuggling operation, and they knew he'd done an 18-month stretch for putting one man in the hospital. They didn't know until January 1993 that they were watching a killer on the loose.

Within weeks, two major developments changed everything. The RCMP smashed the Bahamas cocaine conspiracy, and they found Kungel's skeletal remains. In the Bahamas case, they swooped in on the major players, capturing Austin in Vancouver and seizing drugs worth more than $1 million. They had to be content to issue a warrant for the courier's arrest. They couldn't find him. That was on March 3, 1993.

Their operation had a huge bonus. With the formidable Austin behind bars on a major smuggling conspiracy, Dickson felt safe enough to lead police to Kungel's gravesite. When the RCMP recovered Kungel's remains on March 10 and then kept the discovery secret for weeks, Dickson was the only other person who knew what was going on.

Prosecutors decided Austin's murder trial would take place first, with the Bahamas cocaine conspiracy to follow. In December 1993, Austin stood in the dock before a jury at the Calgary Court of Queen's Bench as a parade of witnesses told the story of Kungel's death.

Kungel's former common-law spouse told the jury that Kungel had left a bag containing $10,000 at her home a short while after $10,000 had been stolen from Austin's house. Then Austin's two musclemen told the jury how they grabbed the fleeing Kungel from a taxi during his attempt to escape them. One of the torturers in the warehouse then testified that Austin had "been enjoying himself" as he sadistically beat and burned his victim.

Fred Dickson told how he and his half-brother Darryl had helped to dig Kungel's grave and that Darryl had later disappeared. He testified that he was one of the four men who took the heavily bandaged Kungel from the warehouse. Dickson said he witnessed Austin shoot and stab Kungel to death at Sibbald Flats and told how he had helped fill in the grave afterwards. Dickson, who had co-operated with and assisted the RCMP, was granted immunity from prosecution.

The jury heard from three of the four witnesses who'd watched Austin execute his victim. The only witness they didn't hear from was the half-brother who'd mysteriously disappeared. Justice was delayed for weeks when Austin's lawyer, Chris Evans, was hit by influenza, and the trial was adjourned until January 1994 to enable him to recover. When the trial resumed, Evans had his chance to attack the credibility of the prosecution's major witnesses. He pointed out to the jury that the three main witnesses had criminal records, were "unsavoury characters" and were lying, as Austin had "nothing to do with" the murder. "They stood up there and took an oath," Evans told the jury, "I'm surprised the testament didn't fly out of their hands."

But the five men and seven women on the jury didn't think the witnesses were lying. They found Austin guilty of first-degree murder, and he was sentenced to life in prison with no chance of parole for 25 years. In sentencing him, Justice Robert Montgomery described the crime as "abhorrent and heinous."

Five months later, Austin was hauled out of prison to stand in the dock again, this time charged with conspiring to import and traffic cocaine from the Bahamas to Canada. The court heard that the ring handled $2.5 million in drugs. This time, Austin pleaded guilty to all charges. Once again the evidence was punctuated by examples of Austin's reign of terror over all those who crossed his path. One man, who Austin reckoned was a leak in his organization, ended up in hospital with his mouth slashed, lacerations, rope burns and a broken arm. And, of course, Darryl Milligan was still missing.

Justice William Egbert sentenced Austin to 15 years in prison. He said Austin used "violence and intimidation" to rule his cocaine distribution ring. "People like him are the dregs of society and should be treated with the contempt they so richly deserve," he said.

Austin tried appealing the court rulings, but to no avail. In February 1996, the Supreme Court of Canada rejected his appeal against the first-degree murder conviction. It was a particularly bad year for Austin. In December, he was brought out of prison to face new charges. This time he pleaded guilty to money laundering and hiding the profits from his drug dealing. These charges earned him an additional 5-year prison sentence. However, under Canadian law the 15-year stretch and the 5-year term have to be served concurrently, as the law prohibits the extra years being tacked on the end of the life sentence. The added blow for Austin was that the court ordered him to forfeit most of his personal property and cough up $40,000 in cash.

One amazing twist in the Kungel murder case had helped defeat Austin. When police were at the crime scene gravesite at Sibbald Flats they knew whose skeleton they were expecting to discover. But would forensic scientists be able to identify him after three years in the ground, especially after Austin's men had poured lime over the body to speed up decomposition? As it turns out, one kind of lime accelerates the decay of a body, but another kind tends to preserve it. Austin's men chose the wrong lime. They had inadvertently assisted the crime scene investigators by helping to preserve Kungel's body.

10

Haunted by Guilt

WILMA BROWN HAD NEVER BEEN so happy. Tomorrow, she was leaving Calgary with her husband and their two teen-aged boys for a vacation to see her relatives in Trinidad, her birthplace. Her folks in Trinidad in the West Indies were just as excited. They couldn't wait for her to arrive.

Les Brown, Wilma's husband of 16 years, went off to work early that morning as he always did. Today he was happy. In just a few hours he'd be on vacation, relaxing on a beach in Trinidad under a tropical sun, far away from the ice, snow and wind chill of Calgary. At 7:30 a.m. the phone rang in his office. It was one of his sons, sounding extremely agitated and upset. Apparently, Mom hadn't turned up for work, and she wasn't anywhere at home. She had suddenly disappeared. It was the start of a nightmare for Les that would last for years, and it led to an almost unbelievable ending.

Wilma worked as a loans manager for the Bank of Nova Scotia in Calgary. Les checked there to confirm for himself that she hadn't shown up for work. She hadn't. He asked the neighbours. None of them had seen her. Growing ever more worried, he contacted her friends, but they hadn't heard from her that day either. Finally, desperate, he reported Wilma as a missing person to Calgary city police. That was March 25, 1982.

Officers in the missing persons unit have heard all kinds of reasons why attractive women go missing. Wilma was 37 years old and definitely attractive. From all the inquiries police made, it was obvious she and Les had been happily married for 16 years. There had been no major problems be-tween them in all that time, and she was a devoted mother to her two sons. But police had known such cases before. A wife becomes bored with her routine life and finds a new man who injects excitement into her humdrum existence. Police files were full of cases where "happily" married women had gone away with lovers. Often, police tracked down the errant wife. Once they were satisfied she was alive, safe and well, their job was done. If the wife didn't want to go home, it wasn't their job to make her go. She was simply removed from the missing persons list.

In this case, Wilma had taken with her the airline ticket for Trinidad and a suitcase full of presents, which she'd

Haunted by Guilt

packed ready to give to her relatives when she arrived. She had left behind her extra clothing and all her valuable and beautiful jewellery.

In the first few days after Wilma disappeared, checks with the airport showed that she hadn't used her airline ticket, but as she'd taken the presents with her, Les believed that she must have decided to go to Trinidad on her own. It seemed he was right when, six weeks after Wilma went missing, rumours circulated that she had been seen in Port of Spain, the island's capital. Les contacted her brother who lived in the United States, and at the end of April the brother went to Trinidad. He searched all over Port of Spain for her with no success.

Les was desperately anxious. His two sons, aged 15 and 13, were taking the disappearance of their mother "very hard," and he was sure the answer to the mystery must lie somewhere on the Caribbean island. When police were interviewing friends and neighbours as part of their missing persons inquiry, everyone said Wilma had been extremely excited about her upcoming visit to Trinidad. In July, three months after Wilma's brother had searched in vain, Les travelled to Trinidad and scoured the island from one end to the other. He too drew a blank.

City police called in Interpol, as it had resources to hunt for people in other countries, but Interpol had no more success than Wilma's brother or Les. As the efforts to find Wilma dragged on without results, it was too painful for Les

125

and the boys to remain living in Calgary in the house from which she had disappeared. To make it easier for his sons to cope, Les moved them to North Vancouver.

By September, when Wilma had been gone for six months, police decided a new blaze of publicity might prompt someone to come forward with information. One story appeared under the headline: DISAPPEARANCE BAFFLES POLICE—DEVOTED MOTHER VANISHES. Constable Bob Hancock, the co-ordinator of missing persons, said foul play wasn't suspected, but it was "out of character" for this religious and devoted mother not to have contacted her family in all this time. It ended with a carefully worded appeal from Hancock, which gave a clue as to what police really thought had happened. He asked for anyone with information to contact Calgary police. "Her location will not be revealed to her family by police if she requests it to remain confidential," he said. Here was the way out for anyone in whom Wilma may have confided. If she had a new life somewhere else that a confidant knew about, he or she could tell police, and Wilma's secret would remain intact. At least then she would no longer be a missing person.

In January 1983, ten months after she disappeared, Wilma's missing persons file was handed over to the city police homicide unit, almost as a routine step. Staff Sergeant Ray McBrien, the head of homicide, said his squad was now dealing with the case because the missing persons unit "has done everything they can, but can't trace her."

In the next few years, Calgary's homicide unit was busy with scores of murders, shootings, stabbings and beatings, but they had nothing new in Wilma's case. She had dropped out of the newspapers for six years, forgotten and just another name added to the long, sad list of women known to be missing across western Canada.

But on April 8, 1988, something amazing happened. Police officers descended on a copse of trees on a remote property many miles north across the Saskatchewan prairies. They were obviously preparing to go digging among the trees. What was most peculiar was that here in Saskatchewan two of Calgary's top homicide detectives were in charge of whatever was taking place. A shovel dug into the earth struck metal only a foot under the surface. Carefully, the soil was scraped away from the metal, and in a few hours the police had retrieved a fridge from under the ground. The detectives believed they had found Wilma Brown in this lonely field, 16 kilometres northwest of the farming hamlet of Shellbrook and 275 kilometres north of Saskatoon. The fridge was opened in the medical examiner's office in Saskatoon, and they found a woman's skeleton inside, tightly wrapped in plastic. A forensic pathologist later confirmed the skeleton was all that remained of Wilma Brown.

How did the Calgary detectives know where their crime scene was? Who told them about the exact location amongst dense trees on a remote parcel of land hundreds of kilometres away from Calgary? Who told them to look for Wilma's six-year-old gravesite in another province?

The dramatic breakthrough had begun two days earlier and two provinces away in British Columbia. A dishevelled wreck of a man, a bum from skid row, smelling badly and looking frail and sickly, walked into a police station. He'd been beaten up and robbed, and he looked badly battered. He started by reporting the robbery—then he started talking about something else. He told an amazing story. He said he could tell police where the body of a woman was buried. Not only was she buried in a shallow grave, but she was also entombed inside a fridge that was under the ground on a remote piece of land in northern Saskatchewan.

The police listened intently. It wasn't the kind of story they heard every Wednesday afternoon. The drunk from the street seemed to know a great many details of this strange story he was telling. Finally, he said he could take them to the field and direct them to where the fridge was buried. The officers took the details and detained him. His name was Leslie Charles Brown, and he'd just informed them that the reason he knew where the body was buried was because it was his wife, Wilma, inside that fridge—and because he had put her there.

Now, after six years of inactivity, the wheels of justice slammed into high gear. Officers in the North Vancouver station where Les was being held contacted the Calgary homicide unit. Two Calgary detectives travelled west on

Thursday, fetched Les and escorted him back to Calgary. Detective Wayne Lauinger of the Calgary police homicide unit and his partner flew with Les to Prince Albert. There, they picked up a team of RCMP officers and forensic crime scene investigators and drove northwest as Les guided them.

Many years later, Detective Lauinger recalled how Les had taken them to a secluded parcel of land, massively over-grown and dense with trees. Way back in the trees was a place where broken branches lay in a pile. It was a scrappy, rough wasteland of trees and rubbish and seemed to have been used as a dumpsite. A derelict old car was lying nearby, upside down and rusting into the undergrowth. They moved the old tree branches from where Les said he had stacked them six years earlier. "We gave Leslie the shovel and he dug. He hit the fridge with his first strike, it was only a few inches down under the surface," said Detective Lauinger.

Then the crime scene investigators took over. From the moment the shovel hit the fridge, the whole area became a crime scene. The forensic officers began carefully sifting the earth away from the fridge until it became obvious there was no evidence to be obtained from the soil around it. Then they called in a front-end loader to dig the fridge out of the ground, its door still tied firmly shut with the heavy rope Les had bound round it all those years before. By the time police had finished at the scene that Friday, they knew that every word Les had told them so far was true. Les, then aged 49, was charged with improperly interfering with a dead body and kept in custody until his first court appearance.

Wilma Brown's story was back in the newspapers, this time splashed across the front page under banner headlines: MISSING WOMAN BURIED IN FRIDGE—SIX-YEAR MYSTERY LEADS TO GRISLY FIND. Shellbrook RCMP constable Greg Heck filled in one small detail—Les Brown's mother owned the acreage where the fridge was discovered. A few days later, Les was released on $1,000 bail, and he returned to his mother's farm in Saskatchewan, where he lived until the case came to trial.

In the months that followed, forensic scientists, crime scene investigators, homicide detectives and Crown lawyers studied the evidence. Saskatchewan's chief coroner, Dr. Diane Stephenson, said the cause of death couldn't be determined because of the state of the "skeletal remains." But finally it was decided there was enough evidence to charge Les with manslaughter. His trial opened on November 6, 1989, in Calgary's Court of Queen's Bench before Justice Russell Dixon. The prosecution outlined a story of homicide and a massive tangle of lies and deceit to cover up the killing. From the mouths of a host of witnesses, including those who'd heard Les Brown's confessions, the judge put the true story together.

It started the night before the Brown family was to leave for Trinidad. That evening, Wilma told her husband she intended to leave him and stay in Trinidad after their vacation. When he and the boys returned to Calgary, it would be without her. The couple had argued in the bedroom over this. Wilma wouldn't tell Les why she was going to leave him and the boys and remain in Trinidad. Les told her he wouldn't let her back in the bed until she explained why.

He then pushed her away. Wilma went backwards over a bedroom chair, which toppled over. She struck her head on a sharp corner and began crying. Les went back to sleep. When he woke later, still in the early hours of the morning, Wilma had obviously climbed back into bed. She was lying there dead and there was blood on the pillow. Right then and there he decided to cover up Wilma's death and make it look like she'd walked out on him. That's what he told Constable William Braes on the day he walked into the North Vancouver police station and confessed.

Silently, without his two sons hearing, Les moved Wilma's body into a storage compartment under the stairs in the basement of their northwest Calgary home and went off to work at his usual time. Then he feigned surprise when he got the first phone call in his office from his son saying Wilma had disappeared. Throughout the day he called neighbours and Wilma's relatives and friends, building the deception that he was frantically searching for his wife who'd suddenly vanished. He even added to the deception by calling police to report her missing. Les kept up the charade for the first week, all the time knowing her body was down in the basement under the stairs.

After a week, it became clear to Les the body wouldn't remain undetected much longer, so he moved her from the basement. He wrapped her body in plastic and placed it in a refrigerator. Amazingly, when he found he couldn't lift the fridge with Wilma inside it, he went and fetched a neighbour. He explained that the fridge had broken down and he needed help to carry it to his truck, so he could take it to be repaired. The neighbour was only too pleased to help, and in no time the fridge, with its door roped shut, was on the truck. The neighbour watched Les drive it off, ostensibly to the repair shop. Instead, he placed it far away from the house in a city storage unit for the next three months.

All this time, Les maintained the appearance of a distraught husband whose wife had disappeared. He even let neighbours know that he'd consulted a psychic, in the hope that assistance from the supernatural world would find Wilma. To prove how earnestly he was searching, he persuaded Wilma's brother to hunt for her in Trinidad and eventually went to the Caribbean himself, ostensibly looking for her.

Les had told neighbours that when he saw how devastated his sons were without their mother, he decided to take them to their grandmother in Saskatchewan. That wasn't the real reason. It was all part of the cover-up plan. His real purpose was that he'd decided an old acreage his parents owned would be an ideal site to bury the fridge and its dreadful secret. While the boys were with Grandma, Les took the fridge and secretly buried it. It took him hours with a shovel to dig a hole big enough. Then he slid the fridge off the back of his truck and dropped it in the hole, filled the hole and covered it with a pile of broken tree branches.

When the boys testified at their father's trial, they both remembered the fridge going with them on the trip to Grandma's farm. Each recalled that their father said he had to deliver it to someone in Saskatchewan when they got there, and they'd thought no more about it.

But their father thought more about it. After he'd taken the boys to live in North Vancouver, he couldn't get the terrible secret out of his mind. The guilt that he'd killed his own wife and knowing what he'd done with her body plagued him every day. His appalling secret drove him to drink. Since the day she lay dead in bed beside him, he had never once spoken a word to anyone about what he had done. As drinking took over his life, his guilty conscience gnawed away at him. His lifestyle deteriorated, and over the years he slumped from being a successful businessman to becoming a pathetic drunk. Still, he kept his secret.

Then things got worse. He was thrown out of his apartment as his life spiralled downwards under the ever-worsening impact of chronic alcoholism. He lost 60 pounds, and finally, after six years of mental torment, he could stand it no longer. On that fateful afternoon of April 6, 1988, when he'd been beaten up and his life was at its lowest ebb, he walked into the North Vancouver police station and unburdened himself. Constable Braes told the judge he gave the appearance of a man who had "fallen from a successful position to a skid row bum." He was gaunt, unshaven, soiled and smelled awful. "I got the impression the guilt had gotten the better of him," said Braes.

The story poured out of Les Brown that day. "I just gotta get this thing straightened around, get it off my chest," he said. "I just gotta pay my penance." He said he'd covered up his wife's death for the sake of his sons. "I didn't want them to know that their daddy killed their mom," he told police. "I didn't mean to kill her. I didn't even mean to hurt her."

After telling police everything he had done with his wife's body and leading them to the exact spot where they could find the buried fridge, Les was allowed to speak to his sons and tell them what he had done. His eldest son testified at the trial that his father told him he thought the death of his wife was "more or less an accident," and that when he pushed her backwards she toppled over a chair and hit her head. The son said his father had staged the entire six-year cover-up for the sake of the boys, to save them from knowing what had happened. "He said he was doing it for my brother and me, so he could raise us and let us grow up."

The judge didn't believe there was anything accidental about it, or that the cover-up was aimed at saving the boys from the truth. He said the cover-up was to save Leslie Brown. The judge convicted Les of the manslaughter of his wife and of improperly interfering with her body, and sentenced him to six years' imprisonment, four for the killing and two for burying Wilma's body in a fridge.

In convicting Les Brown, Justice Dixon said he'd downplayed his involvement in his wife's death when he confessed to police. "Brown did not fully disclose in his statement the severity in which he pushed his wife," said the judge. "There is an intentional brutality." But Alberta's Court of Appeal thought the judge had gone over the top. When Les Brown's appeal against his sentence was heard, his prison term was cut from six to two years. The three appeal court judges agreed with his lawyer, who had argued that the trial judge had based the six-year term not only on the facts, but also on the judge's suspicion that something more than an accidental push had killed Wilma. He also claimed that the original judge hadn't given Les enough credit for turning himself in and confessing when no one in six years had even suspected he had anything to do with his wife's death.

With Les Brown behind bars paying his penance, the case left some crime scene questions unanswered. A decomposing body tends to smell terribly. How had he managed to keep his wife's body concealed in the basement of their family home for a week without the boys detecting it? When he reported Wilma missing, police had visited the house to question him. Were his nerves so ice-cool that he could invite police inside, knowing his wife's body was in the basement as they interviewed him upstairs? Luckily for him, police had no strong reason to suspect him and therefore no reason to apply for a search warrant for the house. And when he placed the fridge in storage for three months, where it obviously wasn't plugged in, did no one detect any strange odours?

How could a father have nerve enough to drive his sons to Grandma's house, many hours away, with a fridge containing their mother's body sitting in the vehicle beside them? Les Brown did all these things and got clean away with killing his wife—except that his conscience haunted him. It took six years, but guilt reduced him to a wreck of a man before he finally confessed. Detective Lauinger said that police could have searched the area around those trees in Saskatchewan forever and never found where the fridge was buried. If Les hadn't talked, the disappearance of Wilma Brown would never have been solved.

Author's Note

There is no bibliography for this book, as none of these cases has appeared in any previously published book. All 10 mysteries and murders are cases that I worked on as the crime reporter for the *Calgary Sun*.

I was the reporter whose exclusive scoop broke the story of the Ted Gawron case, when no one in Medicine Hat had any clue it was happening under their noses. Also, I was at the scene when Ted's remains were discovered in his backyard. I was there the day they dug up Sherwin Fettig from his makeshift grave west of Calgary, and I joined the search for little Jesse Rinker before they found his remains west of Rocky Mountain House. I was at the sewage plant where they found Albert Boudreau's bones and was on the steps of the Canmore courthouse when Jason (Jacob) Lee forgave the media.

To research the other cases, I interviewed family members, lead investigators in the homicide unit and forensic scientists. Over the years, I have saved my notebooks, newspaper cuttings, murder files and court records that provided the original research material for these stories.

Index

Acknowledgements

I would like to thank the many police officers across Alberta with whom I worked on the cases documented in this book during my years as a crime reporter with the *Calgary Sun*. They helped me with inside information about these crimes and mysteries. Many of these officers were with the Calgary Police Service. Especially, I want to thank all the "secret sources" among them, who have had to remain anonymous at all times. You know who you are!

I would particularly like to thank two former Calgary city police homicide detectives, Wayne Lauinger and Allan Hargreaves, who gave me their time and took the trouble to share their memories of the roles they played in two of these cases. I also appreciate the time given me by celebrated anthropologist Dr. Owen Beatty in analyzing the background to the Septic Tank Sam case, on which he had been consulted by police years earlier. I am also greatly indebted to Nicole Giasson, the editor of the *Tofield Mercury* newspaper, and Kathy Levesque of the *Edmonton Sun* library, who worked hard to uncover a wealth of newspaper cuttings for me about Septic Tank Sam.

Thanks once again to my wife, Amanda, who has endured my talk about human skulls, skeletons, murders and torture while I was writing the book. And thanks for allowing our house to be filled from study to attic with my murder files, notebooks and newspaper cuttings. Her computer skills have again been invaluable in saving me when parts of the book were in danger of disappearing into cyberspace forever.

About the Author

Peter B. Smith lives with his wife on Quadra Island, British Columbia, where he retired after a 37-year career as a newspaper crime reporter. He was the crime reporter for *The News* in Portsmouth, England, for 21 years, where he was on call with all three emergency services—fire, police and ambulance—covering thousands of stories of death and destruction. After immigrating to Canada in 1987, he was the crime reporter at the *Calgary Sun* for 16 years, retiring in 2003.

Peter has received numerous accolades, including awards for his coverage of the massacre at the Columbine High School in Littleton, Colorado. Peter also travelled to England to cover the story of Dr. Harold Shipman, the physician who murdered 216 of his patients.

To satisfy his two main interests in life, sea fishing and stamps, Peter ran a twice-weekly sea-angling column for 10 years in England and wrote more than 600 columns for stamp collectors in the *Calgary Sun*, spanning 13 years and earning a national Canadian philatelic literary award.

Peter's first Canadian true-crime book, *Prairie Murders: Mysteries, Crimes and Scandals*, is also published by Heritage House. His previous works include *Sea Angling in Southern England* and the official history of the Portsmouth (England) Fire Brigade, *Go To Blazes*, as well as a specialist stamp book called *Vanuatu's Postal History—The First Decade*. Peter is currently working on a history of the postal service, post offices and postmasters on the tiny islands around his Quadra Island home.

More Great Books in the Amazing Stories Series

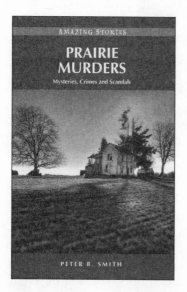

Prairie Murders

Mysteries, Crimes and Scandals

Peter B. Smith

print ISBN 978-1-894974-71-4
ebook ISBN 978-1-926936-26-0

Greed, madness, revenge and political doctrine are but a few of the motives behind eight dramatic prairie murder cases related by author Peter Smith. A Saskatchewan farmhouse is burned to the ground to conceal the brutal murders of a family of seven; a German prisoner-of-war camp in Medicine Hat is the scene of savage Nazi killings; and three desperadoes from Manitoba flee across the prairies and finally engage in a deadly shootout with Mounties near Banff. These are just some of the true tales that explore the dark side of 20th-century prairie history.

Visit heritagehouse.ca to see the entire list of books in this series.